Y0-CBI-562

The Haven

RICHARD DUBÉ

THE HAVEN

HarperCollins*Publishers*Ltd

The Haven
Copyright © 2002 by Richard Dubé
All rights reserved. No part of this book may be used or reproduced in any manner whatsoever without prior written permission except in the case of brief quotations embodied in reviews. For information address: HarperCollins Publishers Ltd., 55 Avenue Road, Suite 2900, Toronto, Ontario, Canada M5R 3L2

www.harpercanada.com

HarperCollins books may be purchased for educational, business, or sales promotional use. For information please write: Special Markets Department, HarperCollins Canada, 55 Avenue Road, Suite 2900, Toronto, Ontario, Canada M5R 3L2

First edition

―――――――――――――――――――――――――

Canadian Cataloguing in Publication Data

Dubé, Richard
The Haven / Richard Dubé.

ISBN 0-00-639162-1

1. Dubé, Richard. 2. Millhaven Institution. 3. Prisoners—Canada—Biography. 4. Murderers—Canada—Biography. I. Title.

HV9505.D82A3 2002   365'.6'092   C2002-902531-1

OPM 9 8 7 6 5 4 3 2 1

To Shari

Contents

Introduction ix

1   Into the Abyss   1
2   My Wasteland   11
3   Goon Squads   17
4   Gated   32
5   Beaver Tail Justice   40
6   Roger Dodger   45
7   Olympic Knockout   50
8   Big Jean   58
9   High School Daze   65
10   Crossing Over   70
11   Crash Test Dummy   78
12   Sentenced   86
13   Prison Prey   92
14   Codes of Conduct   104
15   Taken Down   116
16   Arraigned   128
17   I'll Get Mine   135

18   Eviction Notice   145

19   Lawyers' Games   153

20   Judgment Call   162

21   Protect the Weak   174

22   First Impressions
       of the Haven   183

23   The Jungle Range   191

24   True Colors   202

25   My Ticket to Millhaven   211

26   Inside Millhaven   219

27   Learning the Ropes   233

28   Time in the Big House   243

29   The Parole Hearing   250

30   An Angel   259

Epilogue   271
Acknowledgments   272

Introduction

My story begins in solitary confinement at Millhaven super-maximum-security penitentiary.

The book uses three voices. The main narrative triggers fantasies and flashbacks. Such fantasies are detaching mechanisms commonly adopted by thousands of cons serving hard time. They appear in italics in the book and begin in Chapter 1, "Into the Abyss." The flashbacks are real memories, the first of which also occurs in Chapter 1. The flashbacks begin with a boldface heading.

I spent years inside the infamous mechanical monstrosities. There I came to realize that the majority of hardened and dangerous cons are incarcerated because of substance-abuse problems.

We, the callous killers and calculating robbers, are nothing more than addicts and alcoholics. Now dangerous and demented, we're caught in a vicious cycle: getting stoned, committing crimes and landing in jail, only to come out and do it all over again and again and again.

We, the robbers and killers, follow typical pathways into addiction, and denial is the common denominator. We begin to experiment by smoking pot and hash. We consume large quantities of beer and drink more than our fair share of hard liquor. Some of us get into heavy drugs like cocaine, heroine, ice, crystal, speed, acid and crack. And of course we have those who add to the toxic mix by popping prescription and non-prescription pills.

What's the result? We drop out or are tossed out of school. Some live in turmoil at home, while many others are thrown out and end up on the street, stealing to survive. Some of us work for a living but jeopardize our jobs by partying, scamming, fighting and manipulating others.

Young people are more vulnerable to addiction because their bodies are not fully mature. Beer is more powerful today than it was in the 1980s, up from five percent to seven and a half percent alcohol. Meanwhile, a recently developed cocaine derivative, crack, is one of the most addictive street drugs ever. We understand only when it's too late that youth, alcohol and other drugs make a potent cocktail. Without realizing it, we become addicted. Drinking and taking drugs without ever attempting to control our intake, we don't know if we can. Never trying to quit, we don't know if we can.

I know this in a way that few people do, as my story will show.

The Haven

1

Into the Abyss

Solitary confinement, Millhaven, 1987
I'm sore, stiff and freezing. My bones ache. The hard steel of my chains bites my flesh. I was thrown halfway across my cell when the spray slammed into my naked flesh, and my body is soaked by the icy water fired from the powerful fire hose. The burning sting of mace has subsided, but my sight remains blurry. The cold cement floor numbs my shivering body. I can't straighten up.

I shut my eyes and try to forget the cold. A disjointed volley of images shoot through my mind . . . bright Vancouver sun burning above . . . myself, dark, somber and angry . . . feeling the cool steel of my nine-millimeter . . . pumped and pissed . . . determined and desperate . . .

British Columbia, a few months earlier, 1987
Tense, sweating, heart palpitating, I step into the motel and feel the cold hard steel of my nine-

millimeter pistol swell beneath my black leather jacket. I'm ready to kill or be killed. That's the way it is. Damn straight, man. Any day is a good day to die. I don't give a damn about anything anymore. I've got nothing to lose, and either the cops are going to die or end it for me. That's the least they can do after screwing me over for all of these years.

I approach the little old lady at the desk and demand money. Trembling, she withdraws a small amount from her float as I watch her press the silent alarm beneath the counter. I pretend I don't notice and make my way out into the bright afternoon sunlight. The showdown is about to begin. We're going to shoot it out. I hope I can take a few of them with me before I go down in a flurry of alloy and lead.

I make my way into a small wooded area near a children's playground and reflect on what I'm about to do. I take a moment to sit, and depression weighs heavy as I push the end of the barrel hard against the roof of my mouth and fight for the will to pull the trigger. Unable to go through with it, I emerge from the woods, only to confront a battery of uniformed police.

Blue and red lights flash in all directions. Car doors are flung open and become human body shields. Powerful shotguns equipped with scopes rest on rooftops, while pistols poke through rolled-down car windows. There have to be fifty guns trained on me, any of which could begin blasting away any second. I know when one cop starts shooting, the rest will follow.

Must be fifteen, twenty police cars and fifty or more coppers. Squinting through the glare of the sun, I hear a voice bellow from a hand-held microphone, "Put your hands up and get down on your knees." Looking over to my left, I see a nervous policeman, standing twenty feet away, aim his gun at my chest with a trembling hand. "Drop," he says, through grim lips.

Reaching inside my jacket, I feel the cool steel of my fully loaded semi-automatic. The piece is loaded with ten rounds of explosive power. Blotting out the futility of my situation, I pull the ridged butt of my gun partway out of my jacket and look straight down the barrel of the cop's .38. His hands are trembling and I swear I can smell the black alloy's killing power. The sound of countless shotguns loading echoes in the empty playground, driving home the fatal nature of my situation.

I feel calm and at peace with the universe. This is the end. I can't go on living. It would be better if I could take a few of them with me, but I'll never get any of them now. I should have killed them when I had the chance.

The guns remain firmly trained on me. One more move and I'm gone, and I know it. They'll blow so many holes through me, I'll look like the fountain of youth.

The cops remain motionless. Why aren't they shooting? My gun is half exposed and the trigger-man has cocked the hammer on his piece. He'll blast me between the eyes. But I sense he doesn't want to. What's his problem?

He's a damn kid. He's terrified. He doesn't want to know what killing does to your mind. I know what killing feels like . . .

The henchmen from Hades have damaged me beyond repair. The pricks. I can't relate to these doorknobs and straight johns out here. Can't get a damned job . . . no money . . . no future . . . no hope. I've lost the capacity to love, to care and to be at peace.

What's the sense in going on? Nothing has any meaning . . . everything is a game with people playing rote roles. I exist in an empty cosmos, traveling through this wasteland with murderous rage as my only constant. I can't go on like this.

Life's overvalued . . . it's a death sentence . . . a burden to bear . . . a hellish dimension imposed without my consent . . . I've been catapulted into the realm of insanity and can't reverse the damage, but my vision is clear and my mind is lucid.

The bastards have rendered me culturally illiter-ate . . . I don't fit in anywhere . . . I'm lost. Unforgiving bastards, the whole lot of them. They impose value judgments on me, but I'm much more aware than any of these idiots. I understand the forces that mold a character and the dynamics that sculpt a personality.

I've not wasted all of my time in the infamous mechanical monstrosities. I could write a dissertation on the criminal. I've had plenty of time to evaluate myself, but also lots of time to examine the world's injustices.

I never asked for alcoholic parents or an older brother who became a hardened criminal and sociopath. I never planned to drink, and certainly never dreamed of committing crimes, but the blueprint was already drafted. Everything I did, though, I did while I was drunk. You pricks were sober when you abused, tyrannized and oppressed me for those days, weeks, months and years.

Schools threw me out; teachers thought I was just plain bad. They never heard the battles in my home late in the evenings when the drunkards came back from the tavern. Courts, lawyers and judges never took time to intervene. And once you're in the clutches of the criminal justice system, the stigma, coupled with people's prejudices, seals your fate. They'd have me working as a grocery clerk when I'm bilingual and university-educated.

Oh, yes, I made the choices, but what kind of

choices is a fatherless, alcohol- and drug-addicted teen going to make? What the fuck was I supposed to do?

I was destined to end my life this way . . .

The biting cramp in my leg smashes into my mind like an unwelcome intruder. Reality reminds me that I should have let them kill me. Death would be better—*anything* would be better—than this.

Trying to ease the pain, I inch my way into a new position. The bastards have left me in a puddle of water. Stinky, freezing, dirty water that leaves me numb and shivering. My skin is turning blue. It's been hours since I last ate, and it's hours more to go. I try to ignore the physical torment. Time goes by too damn slow.

Moments crawl . . . minutes feel like hours, hours like days . . . amid the deafening silence . . . dead silence for days . . . interminable. Seconds turn into minutes . . . and another . . . and another . . .

My recurring fantasy
of revenge in the hole at Millhaven

Majestic old-growth giants stretch proudly into the gilded horizon and converge on snow-tipped mountain peaks puncturing swirling wisps of clouds. I'm mesmerized by the lull of the watery azure as the ocean breeze rustles overgrown leaves on umbrella-sized branches. Drawing huge drafts of the sweet aroma of pine, I feel the crisp morning chill caress my red cheeks.

In the distance, a rushing brook weaves a blue ribbon through the pure and clear mountains. Ears trained on the gentle cascade, I hear spring birds announce the arrival of a new season with a dulcet chorale. Nature is so majestic — breathtaking! How I missed her rejuvenating dimensions and yearned for her healing properties. How earnestly I craved to hug my big old tree when I was locked up like a wild beast in Millhaven.

Oh, yes, I was brutalized, tortured and made to suffer. I'll never forget your torture dungeons — those putrid, inhumane testing laboratories. It was horrific; a vivid and brutal nightmare.

As for you sniveling, groveling, vermin-filled maggots, welcome to my nightmare, you sons of bitches. It's payback time. Wait until the guys inside read your missing person reports and see your filthy faces pasted in every tabloid across the country. The boys inside your infamous mechanical beasts will relish the fact that revenge is being exacted — even if the boys in the joint don't know I'm the long-awaited vigilante man.

Let me say that I've accomplished this feat primarily for my selfish satisfaction. Rest assured it includes all of you, so that you too may come to know pain and suffering as I've come to know them. Let us take this delightful opportunity to connect our fields of experience. You'll come to identify and empathize, you pricks.

Can you feel the solitude descending like a suffocating cloud of coal soot? Feel the fire of hatred burn your face like mace? Feel yourselves slipping into the dark abyss of insanity and sliding into the chasm of psychosis? Taste the blood of revenge wetting your filthy palates? You will . . . oh, yes . . . you will.

What a historic coup. Six brutal penitentiary screws, two pig-faced, tyrannical wardens, four abusive and slanderous coppers, one dictatorial, power-driven parole officer, one heavy-handed, closed-minded judge, one cunning and deceiving crown attorney and two filthy rat-bastard enemies. How sweet revenge really is. I never thought I could catch so many of you bumbling idiots, but here you are, buried deep underground in my makeshift prison.

QUIET! QUIET . . . filthy rodents . . . QUIET.

This pit was dug with my own sweat and it took a tremendous amount of effort to carve it into the cold hard ground. Tell me. How do you feel being so deep in this remote wooded area, my dear little prisoners? You know you're doomed and without hope, don't you? Look at the towering pine trees. Right, you can't see from down there.

I'm delighted with my calculations and precise measurements. The fortified bus fits perfectly in the ground I've prepared for it. It had taken long, arduous work to strip the bus of its contents. The steel-barred ceiling and cast-iron walls and floor have been masterfully laid. No amenities for you whimpering, low-life cowards. You can see this ingenious creativity as my version of your Chinese cell. I spent many days in the cells with nothing but a hole in the floor as a toilet. What was I supposed to learn in those bare concrete holes? To hell with all of you. As you can see, you're not the only ones who can build torture pits and insane asylums.

Keep sniveling and groveling; I don't give a shit. In fact, your unceasing lamenting and frightened cries are music to my ears.

How long I have waited for this moment of triumph. Seven long years . . . yes . . . seven long years of careful planning and six months of hard, dedicated work— and here it is. Incredible. I bet you're incredulous yourselves. Well, you better start believing. How long did you think you could keep on antagonizing and oppressing me before fate turned on you? Do you think I'm some kind of laboratory rat devoid of reason? Nobody messes with me. Suit or no suit. Law or no law.

We're all human and we all bleed . . .

Faint voices echo in the corridor as the sound of jangling keys teases my ears. My mind struggles to focus through the vivid images of my lingering fantasy. A set of heavy footsteps approaches my cell and stops abruptly.

Throbbing . . . my head is pounding, and focusing is difficult. Shaking my head, I try to clear the cobwebs from my mind. A pair of dark eyes peers through the slot of my door and I feel shame in my nakedness. I laugh madly and want to lash out viciously. The dark eyes suddenly fill with terror. The bright light in my cell veils my sight. Everything is so damn unreal. Emptiness envelops me.

2

My Wasteland

Crawl. Drag yourself, Ritchy. Have to get to the door, but these chains and belts leave me paralyzed, immobile.

I've been bound and chained like a beast for over seventy-two hours. Lying on this wet floor, I'm seized with rheumatic aches from head to toe. My murderous rage soothes me; it is my only numbing respite. I need to return to fantasyland, so they better leave me alone. I'll get even very soon. Let them dish it out; it'll come back a hundredfold.

My naked, curled torso is tightening, contracting in the cold air that flows through the cracks around my solid steel door. The chilling vapor wracks every sinew of my cramped body. The callous bastards have left the door leading to the yard open. I'm freezing because of these pigs.

I want to remain, unfeeling and entertained, in my fantasy. These jerks will be cold and shivering some day soon. Law restrains them, but I've adopted my own law. The power is mine, not theirs.

Prying eyes remain fixed on me, so I better not utter a word. I know the barbarians want to send me to their notorious insane asylum in Penetanguishene. The idiots want to send me to that hate factory and keep me doped up. Forget that trip. They're the psychotics, not me.

I drag myself across the floor through my piss. The stench fills my nostrils. I know the men in the hole are becoming sick with it, sick with the nauseating smell of putrid bowels. It smells like death.

I'll stay in this shithole until I'm released onto the street. Then I'll pay a few visits, after I steal my bus, reinforce it and dig my hole deep in the woods. Yes, the plan is almost complete.

The dark eyes look away . . . I hear muffled voices. What the hell are they talking about? Mumbling voices echo off the walls. Is the shrink advising the screws to loosen the restraints and grant me clothes, food, a mattress and maybe a shower? "Don't be such a humanitarian, Doc. You're a collaborator and I know your true colors. You're very close to being put on my hit list. Shut your fat trap and leave while there's still time. Think of your loved ones."

Drag yourself, Ritchy. Have to make it to the door and prepare to get warm and play some music in this whole hellish inferno. The damn floor . . . it's freezing cold ... my aching spine is tight ... rigid. Rheumatism is going to set in for good.

My bare feet are numb. Millions of needle pricks move through my toes. I must ignore the pain and get warm. Have to bang my frozen feet on the hard steel door and send sounds of fury throughout solitary confinement. Lying on my back, I let go the first blow.

Kaboom! I kick the door and a shock of pain reels through my body. The chains and shackles rattle.

Frustrated, I lift my feet and slam them into the door for the second time. Kaboom! The reverberating crash chases the first down the hallway as a wave of pain hits me. Faintly, I hear a few cons follow my example. The piercing, pulsating pain and burning hatred I feel is music to my ears.

I can't continue. My energy sapped, I collapse. I've not eaten in ... in ... three days. The mind is willing, but the body surrenders.

Wandering back through the dark abyss of my mind, I find thinking difficult. What's real and what's fantasy? I can't distinguish any more. Think ... think. Straining, I feel the tight band that constricts my head start to loosen and, slowly, the mental haze lifts ...

Wait until I get my hands on the rat responsible for my being locked up in this shithole, stripped naked, freezing, aching, bound and chained like a wild beast—wanting to kill, murder and mutilate. Just wait. When I get my hands on him, it'll be sweet, better than that other time . . .

Attack in Millhaven yard a few weeks before, 1987

The torrential downpour grants me an ideal time to carry out my deliberate attack. The little punk is going to pay, and pay dearly. Slinking through my rain cover like a thirsting and territorial predator stalking its prey, I weave my way quietly through the steady rain with vicious intent.

I spot my victim strolling casually along the narrow track yard. The little jerk is unaware of my presence, oblivious to his vulnerability. In an instant, he's engulfed by my wrath. I emerge from the rain dripping with anger and about to inflict serious bodily harm. Had he not jeopardized my life only days before?

I know the tower guards are blinded by the downfall. I can't even see the armed screws in their fortified turrets. My target is caught—and hopeless. Under the steady sheet pouring down from the heavens, my victim will plead for his rotten life.

Heart palpitating, blood rushing, with one leap I pounce like a crazed cougar and tackle him to the ground with such force he's knocked almost unconscious. Under the force of the blow, his ribs break and his breath explodes. Rolling on top of him, I sit heavily on his sunken chest as he gasps for air. I pull his dirty-blond locks to the cold hard ground with one hand, while my knees lock his tattooed arms to his sides. I slam the palm of my other hand over his gaping mouth. He's flat on his back and completely powerless.

Glaring into his twisted face through the veil of my fury, I hiss that he's about to die and I'm going to get twenty-five years for it. That's the law of the land—and how problems are dealt with in here. We go to the limit and play for keeps in the Haven.

Lips quivering, he weeps like a child and begs for his life. Eyes burning with anger, I raise my clenched fist a little higher and take careful aim at his throat. That's it for him . . .

The shuffling of many feet jolts me back to the present. What the hell do they think they're doing? My food slot opens and the screw's ugly pockmarked face intrudes on my privacy. I recommend he not remove my cuffs because I'll drive my clenched fists into his face.

Which one will try me? Let them bring four to five of their best and let's fight to the end. I'll break a few bones, but I won't kill anybody purposely—at least not here and now. I'll just kick, punch, knee and elbow a few of them. They'll be hospitalized, but it would be better to take a beating now than to visit my makeshift prison when I get out.

I'm not going back home to Sudbury. I'm moving to Kingston when I'm released, and they can't stop me. I'll go into hiding and catch them all—one at a time.

3

Goon Squads

The dull hum of the automatic opener alerts me the door is opening, revealing five ugly screws. Their fat bellies bulge under dull gray shirts, and I visualize what a smear of freshly spilled blood would look like on their crisp, gray pleated slacks. What, I wonder, would it feel like to drive my hand through their ribs? Ooooooh, how I wish I could slam these rotten screws. I'd go right through them—rip their cold hearts right out.

Hands grapple with me and pull me to my feet. I wish they'd stay away. Where do they think they're taking me? The corridor seems so large, so bright. I can't keep my eyes from squinting in the light, and the powerful smell of medicinal antiseptics clings to my burning nostrils, leaving a bitter aftertaste. The steam from the hot shower across the hall reminds me of the hot cascades the screws will get in *my* prison. Yes, I'll toss caldrons of boiling water on their writhing, naked bodies.

Can't they see I don't care if I shower? I hate their ugly contorted faces. I want to stay locked up and dirty, like an animal, until the doors open for me. I want this memory fresh and I want it to fuel me.

Scalding hot water peels off piss and shit as the heavy chains clang in the cramped metal cubicle. The bastards can clean off my body, but they can never wash out the beast within. Don't they know my mind belongs to me, and my soul is not theirs to tamper with? There are certain dimensions not accessible to others' influence. My spirit is not within their corrupt sphere or anywhere they're acquainted with.

The buckle of the leather restraining belt is cold against my navel and I'm left with little mobility. These sick mothers will have to remove my chains if I'm going to wash my hair and body fully. They'll have to suck up now, as I'm being released in a few days. I know the mad doctor forced them to comply with humane conditions.

The water stops and I push the rounded steel knob for another warm cascade. I can barely reach. On tiptoes, I jump slightly and press the cool knob in. The spray is light, but I'm warming up a bit. I can feel the numbness leave my toes.

The water stops and the screw with flapping jowls and a dark complexion ambles toward my cell. He thinks I'm going to walk back into my pit voluntarily.

To hell with him; he'll have to take me by force. I'm still chained and shackled, but I'm not going back into that suffocating pit. I'm not that institutionalized, nor that tamed and domesticated. I'll never stop seeing this madhouse and these puppet masters for what they are. I'm not some automated, mindless robot. I refuse to go back to my hole, pig.

The brick walls in my tiny quarters simply divide rooms. Nothing more. I see beyond the physical limitations of this beast. I've never failed to see the fences—and see them for what they are. They can restrain the physical, but they can never limit my free spirit.

Three burly screws seize my arms and lift and drag me toward my hole. Furious, I spit in their faces and see terror in their eyes. My body is cleansed, but my heart and mind are polluted. Tensing my body, I try to spread my legs, but the leg irons cut into my ankles. They better get their hands off me or I'll bite the skinny screw's nose off.

Releasing their grip, they attempt to reason with me. Are they nuts? Reason deserted me years ago. Vengeance is my only preoccupation. I'll kill a lot of them. They have tormented me for too long. Their time is coming. The slimeballs won't find me, either. I'll be stealthy and smart.

Can these assholes see what's inside this body and mind? Not a chance. Their crazed eyes regard bulging biceps and striated pectorals. They see a mask of hatred and a figure of madness, but they can't see the depths of my soul.

They wrestle me back into my cell. I hear the door slam shut. I stare blankly at the solid blue metal and smash my fists into its surface. The reverberating echo startles the screws. I feel no pain.

The screws are terrified and not one has the balls to confront me. They're afraid for their lives and I know it. Why were they trying to be reasonable today? Hypocrites; it's too late for niceties. For weeks, months and years, they've treated me callously and provoked me endlessly. I want—and will get—their sweet asses.

The screws march away as I sit on my tiny steel cot. I bet they'll come back and take off my chains, give me food, clothes and bedding. They can only go so far, because I'm going to be released in a few days. Now that's comforting. I'm ready to die for my cause.

Here they come. My door opens. They're so predictable they make me sick. Child's play. The screws burst into my cell and remove my leg irons and the leather restraining belt. Their breath fills my room and makes me sick. Now that I can move, I want to kick the bearded monstrosity in his bulbous nose. I could kill him if I kick him in the throat or drive the bridge of his nose into his pea brain.

The goon squad slowly paces out of my dungeon and the door slams shut with a loud clang. My food slot opens and a scrawny screw asks me to put my hands out so he can remove my cuffs. Sure, why not, full and complete mobility. The cuffs slip off and I smash my fists into the steel blue door. The screw backs away in fear, his eyes registering shock. What if I had connected that shot to the side of his temple? He could die from such a blow. I harbor so much pent-up hatred, I could kill him with one solid punch.

Power surges through my arms, my jaw tightens and my gut twists with anxiety. Every muscle in my body is as taut as steel and ready for battle. My forearms feel like iron bars, my stomach like an oak board, my neck muscles constricted and tense. I can't be hurt—not a chance.

As I pace to and fro like a caged animal, the screws place a neat bundle of clothes on top of the tray of my food slot. They pass me a dirty mop and ask me to clean my living quarters. These weekly cleanups only serve to mask the stench in this hellhole. What the hell, I've been in the hole for forty days already and I need to clean it or risk getting scabies.

The foul odor of dried excrement and urine mixes with rotten food. I've grown accustomed to it, but I have to think of the other cons. They could get sick and contract some disease. I swish the wet mop on yellow brick walls and the dried food I refused to touch peels off. I push the murky water through the crack of my door.

Oh, noooo—not the damn crickets! The suckers are starting again. The little bastards drive me insane. This is more debilitating than any brutality that the screws can administer. I'm forced to do double time. I can't sleep to escape the dreadful reality of my plight. I want to smash something— anything at all. I want to scream, "Bastards, come on. Let's do it—bring in a few of your best and give me a shot at the title." Dodging from side to side, I act out a left jab, a right kick, and a hammer blow to the temple.

The punk in the next cell starts to yap at me. He wants to meet me in the yard and finish a discussion we began a few days ago. He's already killed at least two other men and now he has the balls to threaten me. Ha. What a jerk. I called him and his father an idiot and they didn't say anything. The father and son team backed down when it was time for action. His dad killed some kid on the street and is doing the book, aka twenty-five years. Asshole, it's easy to be tough behind solid steel doors.

Doesn't he know that these walls have ears? What if I kill him in the yard? I'll be caught for sure. He's a punk. Wait until I get my hands on his scrawny frame. I'll break his skinny fingers one at a time. If he continues to threaten me, I'll snap his pointy elbows. If he won't quit, I'll break his ankles.

I won't be able to kill him. I know I'll have to break his nose and his jaw and crack a few of his ribs. But I can't kill him. I have to get out of this zoo and carry out my plan. The punk will be transferred out of this madhouse after I beat him.

My food slot creaks open, and the damn screw asks for my mop. I feel like snapping the handle in half and driving it into his fat gut. Handing me fresh bedding, he leaves a thin mattress outside my door. Do they dare open my door? Do they think I've calmed down? They're extremely stupid. Simpletons. They should have kept me chained and shackled before they brought me a mattress. What a bunch of hypocrites. Do they think being nice now will save their lives? Never.

The screw leaves as my door opens a crack. Then I step into the brightly lit corridor, kick the mattress away and call them on for a fight to the death. I know they're exasperated with me. Three uniforms remain safely behind the steel barrier, where they look on in defeat. If they don't want any more trouble, they should never have lit the fuse.

I'm flipped and I want to fight. They push and torment, and now I need to feel some contact with these jerkoffs. I have to tense up and wrestle with the goons for hours. The screws don't know what to do with me now. I'm no longer restrained and can fight like the devil himself. It had taken the assholes an hour to restrain me the first time—it'll take a lot more this time. I'll never be broken. My will is unbending . . . unyielding . . . unbreakable.

It's always been this way with me. Even as a scrawny kid who hardly knew a damn thing, I knew this much: nobody gives me shit and gets away with it . . .

Home life as a teen, 1974

On a warm summer day, my buddy Dan and I amble nonchalantly into my house. We're thirsty and head for the kitchen. I'm listening to Dan cheerfully relate his favorite play of the baseball game we've just won when he stops abruptly. Stepping into the kitchen, we stumble on my dear mother and the drunk.

Her worn and torn pink housecoat thrown loosely over her stooped shoulder, my mother is hunched over the kitchen sink. Dark mascara streams down her pale, wet cheeks. Her shoulders slumped and shaking, she's choking back tears. I turn and look over at Dan, and my face turns beet red as I feel the heat of shame burn my face.

The unshaven, pot-bellied bastard stands a few paces from my defenseless mother, his eyes crazed and puffed from the long bout of drinking the night before.

My mother becomes more distraught with our unexpected arrival. Fear is inscribed in her meek features. She knows how I feel by the look of contempt I burn into her teary eyes.

She seems so helpless and powerless. How could he do this to her? And why? I snap. My shame gives way to anger.

Turning abruptly to Dan, my face red, my chest tight with anxiety, I tell him to leave. I know Dan has seen me angry before, but never like this.

Shocked, fearful, concerned, Dan refuses to leave. His light blue eyes beg me to leave with him. I flatly refuse and my anger goes up. Looking around the tiny kitchen, discomfort setting in and unsure of what to do next, Dan asks if he can stay in the doorway to the veranda. Gazing intently into his anxious blue eyes, I advise him to "Stay the hell away and do not come close." If he wants to see a real-life, brutal fight scene, he'll be seeing one now. I'm a fourteen-year-old weighing in at 110, and I'm ready to kick the shit out of 240-pound drunk.

Muscles taut in my chest and belly, arms tensed and ready, I clench my fists and my jaw and make my way to a spot between the drunk and my mother. I'm pumped and I'm furious. I feel no fear.

My neck muscles strain from the fury; the drunk

and I begin circling one another. Keeping my eyes
on his face, I cross my feet over one another and
start moving cautiously to his right.

Staring contemptuously at him, shaking with fury,
I hiss threats at his swollen, distorted face. "You fat
prick, that's it. We're not putting up with your
fucking shit anymore. I'm going to kick your ugly
fucking face in . . ."

The smell of liquor on his raunchy breath angers
me even more. The tension mounts steadily as the
drunk looks at me stupidly. I look back intently,
straight into his bloodshot eyes. The bastard won't
back away.

At this point, everyone disappears in my mind's
eye. My concentration honed, I can barely hear anything. His fat gut hangs out over loose-fitting blue
denim jeans. The bastard weaves in my direction. As
my eyes burn into his, my anger and rage multiply.

Circling near the counter, I reach over and grab
an eight-inch kitchen knife out of its wooden
holder. Squeezing the handle into the palm of my
hand, I feel the knuckles of my fingers tighten.

My mother's voice reaches a hysterical pitch that
pulls me out of my concentration. She's freaking.
I'm alarmed and distracted by her hysteria and the
drunk seizes the opportunity to grab hold of my
hand. Very swiftly and powerfully, he turns the
blade toward me. He's a lot stronger than I thought.

I'm shocked and scared. His sweaty palms squeeze my wrist and hand and I can't break the hold. I'm locked and I'm caught. I can't drop the knife or shake his powerful grip.

Both Dan and my mother are yelling and screaming, but I can't hear what they're saying. The point of the blade is inches from my stomach. Everything slows. The sounds in the house . . . their voices . . . they're echoing and my mind is reeling in confusion. My arm is caught, and this is the end.

Suddenly, the heavy pig lunges forward, throwing his entire bulk behind the attempt. I'm forced up against the refrigerator, the blade driving for my guts.

Instinctively, I slide my body slightly to the side. The blade misses my stomach, hits the refrigerator door, snaps cleanly from its short handle and falls to the floor. I'm left holding the small plastic handle.

Shocked, unbelieving, the drunk and I stop—everything is suspended in time. The prick almost killed me.

Trembling, I slowly come to my senses. The drunk is bewildered. I push myself off the refrigerator door. We face each other in the middle of the kitchen. We stand motionless for a few seconds, unsure what to do next. Everything is deathly quiet.

I step back a few feet and turn to look at Dan and my mother. I'm severely shaken. I narrowly escaped being killed. This thing is not turning out right. My stomach is in knots and my mind in a cloud.

Walking over to Dan, I advise him in a trembling voice to leave immediately, as things are going to get "very fucking messy." Looking into my friend's eyes, I declare, "I will kill this big prick one way or another, so you better leave."

Near tears, Dan implores me to leave with him. "No way, Dan, I'm not fucking leaving. I'm going to give it to this fat fucker. The prick is going down."

Without another word, I turn away and make my way to the middle of the kitchen in an attempt to pacify my frantic mother. Between sobs, Mom is mumbling some nonsense. I put my hands on her shoulders and tell her not to move. She's still crying and protesting when I turn away. Her pleas only serve to deepen the anxiety stirring in the pit of my gut.

I see the idiot move to the far side of the room, making a slow retreat into the hallway. The bastard thinks this is over.

Determined, I march toward the beast. I'm soon within two feet of his fat bulging figure. I'm very calm for some reason. I have my attack plan mapped out in my mind.

Thoughts of the many nights my sleep's been disturbed by the crashing of dishes come dancing into my mind. The countless times this piece of shit has

kept me awake and the many times he's made my
mother cry well up in my mind like a hurricane. My
pent-up hatred wells to the surface. I don't care how
big and ugly the bastard is. I have to put a stop to
this fucking bullshit— even if it means getting killed
in the process.

The drunk raises his hands as I close the distance
between us. Reaching under his hairy chin in one
fluid movement, both palms firmly in place, I push
my whole weight off the floor.

His head crashes into the wall with such force our
hanging picture plate almost falls off its mounting.
I'm sure his head is split wide open. Looking into
his cloudy eyes, I watch him slide to the floor with a
loud piercing yelp, his face wincing in pain.

Hovering over his crumbled body, I consider
kicking his face in, but he's not moving. Without
looking at Mom, I stride out of the house . . .

The sound of countless army boots echoes off the
walls, and the image of the fat drunk expands and
then dissolves into a goon squad. Their body-length,
clear-plastic shields, domed headgear, padded vests
and swaying billy clubs create a wall down the hall as
they march in unison. I know this is a psychological
ploy to try and scare me. Do they think such tactics
work? I'm not afraid of their antics and power trips.
Let me show them how to create fear in cold hearts. I

can go right through their flimsy walls. Who'll be the first hero to come within striking distance? Who's willing to lose an eye for the cause? I'll return to my cell when I want to, and not when they tell me.

As they approach, their contorted features peer out from under plastic facemasks. Anxious voices demand I return to my cell, or else . . .

I know their motives are fear and control, so I won't give an inch. The human wall slowly closes the distance. Assuming my side karate stance, my body gets loose and my concentration honed. I throw vicious sidekicks and the all-powerful wall ceases abruptly. Ha. The idiots are scared. They've heard me smash fists against concrete walls and steel doors and know what happened to some cons after fighting me. They're terrified. They know I've never hit any of them before, but today could be differ-ent—one good punch on one of their necks and it could snap like a dry twig.

Approaching ever more slowly, they surround me. Their three-foot-long billy clubs sway dangerously close. Grasping their sticks with padded leather gloves, the goons anxiously wait to find the opening where their weapons can crash against my bones. Turning, I keep an eye and ear on all of them. None moves an inch.

Body tensing, I feel the surge of hatred rush

through my body. I can kill with one punch and I know it.

The small screw with the neatly trimmed black moustache wants to be a hero. I see intent in his dark, hooded eyes; no doubt the coward has a small-man complex. If he swings his club, I'll catch it on my rock-hard stomach and seize his weapon. I'll pull him near, knee him in the ribs, twist his neck and throw him to the floor.

Let the idiot try and hit me. I can't feel a thing anyway. The damn thing will bounce off my body. And he's too damn slow. The little bastard makes a move toward me, and when I feint in his direction, he pulls back his club. I laugh and hiss. Let the coward come and swing his club. I'll snap it and crack it over his empty skull.

I'm still pumped, but the tense standstill ends when I decide I had better return to my cell and not jeopardize my release, due in just a few days. I can't protect myself without incurring charges for assault causing bodily harm. They'll only get the tear gas and mace. As far as I'm concerned, it's good enough to get the cowards down here. And the goons will be called again, so they might as well stay alert.

4

Gated

The mind is a marvelous mechanism, able to endure torture and isolation for so long, the body resilient to pain and the will fortified with fury. Cast away from society, I see life objectively now, not tainted by material distractions or ugly noise. I can turn my eyes inward like Montaigne, St. Augustine and Descartes. I can become a philosopher and address the moral metamorphosis that consumes men in these barbaric dungeons . . . I see and feel it . . .

Human nature is not pure. Men are dark, ugly savages seeking to satisfy their demented penchant for cruelty. What good lies in me? None.

My tiny food slot pops open, yanking me out of my thoughts. A cold meal is served on a thin metal tray. Should I throw it at the jerk or eat it? I'll eat this time; I'm famished. Chewing my stewed beef, I begin to think about how I've come to be here in the first place . . .

Boozing buddies, 1967

King Alcohol is the monarch of our feudal and
feuding family. It's safe to say my mother and her
consort have become shivering denizens of King
Alcohol's mad realm. Soaking their bodies and
minds, it invades our home and brings with it
misery, chaos and heartache.

Draped in its purple pouch and gold ribbon,
Crown Royal is perched in the side door of our beer-
filled refrigerator. Bottles of Molson Export are
stacked atop one another like the bricks of a castle.
There is no room for food. Fruit juice is supplanted
by Molson muscle, brick cheese by rye. Vegetables
and fruits fall to the army of general vodka and mix.
Milk gives way to the maneuvers of crème de
menthe and Bailey's, and so the battle rages.

The insanity in the home is frightful. Coming
home from school for lunch one day, I discover
mom in her housecoat, again with mascara streaked
down her pale face. The house is a veritable mess
and so is she. I'm confused and I don't understand
she's hungover. She's been sick all that morning.

She looks so pitiful and weak. This isn't the mother
I've known all these years. The mother who cradled
me in her tender loving arms is . . . is . . . gone.

Then there are the arguments when dishes
careen and crash on the walls and screaming
matches last into the small hours of the morning. I

awaken in fear and don't know what to think, how to feel or how to act, so I stay firmly wrapped in my blankets, frightened of what's going to happen next.

Looking around my dark room, I ask myself where my big brother Michel is, where my eldest sister Lisette has disappeared to and why my other older sister Monique is no longer around. Poor little Suzanne is in another room, and I wonder if she can hear the fighting too.

Suzanne and I are left alone to contend with King Alcohol and his crazed victims . . .

A brown manila envelope slides under my door. What the hell could it be? I haven't received a letter in years. Ripping it open, I see something from the National Parole Board. Reading the contents carefully, I'm enraged. I can't believe it. The pricks are serious about their intent to "gate" me. They want to keep me locked up until my sentence expires. What I'm looking at is a dangerous offender application. They want to keep me for another eighteen months. What am I going to do?

I was supposed to be out five months ago. The bastards made me redo five months—which is called "double jeopardy." Their sentence calculations and parole regulations are clearly unconstitutional, but I can't get my writ of habeas corpus filed because they're keeping me in the hole.

The screw with the smart mouth and arrogant yuppie face returns and says the judge wants to see me. I'd set fire to the yard a few days ago. Now they want to take me to their kangaroo court. But I'm not going peacefully. They'll have to drag me in and I'll fight every inch of the way. They're just trying to make sure the parole board gates me. It's a setup.

They've tried twice to place me in the special-handling units—those infamous black pits reserved for the most dangerous criminals in the pen. Fortunately, I won those battles.

I have too much on my plate. I'm going to snap at the seams. The pressure is too much. How did it all get started? I'm getting really frustrated and desperate. How am I going to deal with the parole board? What if they gate me? I'm among the "civil dead." I have no rights.

Screw them; they can put it to me one more time. I won't die in this hellhole. Nobody is going to kill me here and I won't jeopardize my freedom by killing another. I have loftier goals. I'm the destined one.

Five burly screws come to my door and it looks like we're going to get down and dirty. The whole sad scene is going to start all over again. Just because of that stool pigeon in the yard. He's lucky to be alive. If he'd stabbed that guy like he was supposed to, I wouldn't have had to enforce the codes we all know so well. Some of these guys talk the talk but can't walk the walk.

My cell door slides open and the goons rush in and grab hold of my arms and my legs. I wriggle and twist and they have a hard time pinning me down. Breathing heavily, the fat, bulging goon with the dark-circled eyes places the mace gun hard against my eye. I spit on his shiny new black boots and invite him to shoot.

They manage to roll me on my stomach and secure my hands behind me. Pulling hard against the steel, I numb the pain out right away. They try to lift me up, but I wrap my leg around the fat porker's thigh. We're caught.

Indignant and very pissed off, they hoist my arms and I'm forced to my toes. My shoulders feel like they're ripping apart. I throw myself into the air and brace my bare feet on the doorframe. They can't push me out. Yanking me violently back inside my cell, they shackle my ankles and hustle me out into the corridor again.

Dragging me twenty yards, a heaving throng of screws wrestles me to the doors to the kangaroo court and lead me inside. They're perspiring and breathing deep, I'm red-faced from straining, and my muscles scream to be let loose. I feel like I've wrestled for hours.

The judge of the kangaroo court looks like an idiot

sitting on his elevated bench as he contemplates me through pop-bottle bifocals. I scream and hurl insults, knowing I'm already guilty in his biased eyes. He never listens to my side. "Stuff it, pencil neck. You look retarded in your ugly brown suit." Peering intently through his thick glasses, he quickly pronounces my fate and adds a few days to my time in the hole. I laugh in his sunken face. I'll serve my time in the hole or in segregation; I really don't care. Eighteen more months—at most.

I'm dragged back and slammed into my dungeon, cuffed and shackled. At least I had a meal, got some clothes. My shithouse is clean and I had a shower. I feel pretty damn good, considering where I am. This is nothing . . . sweet dick all . . . time is time is time.

The skinny mustachioed screw appears at my cell and says he wants my cuffs and shackles removed. They're doing this because of the doc. "Eat this, dickhead, I like the feel of cold hard steel on my body. Come and take them off if you think you're man enough." He looks away. The echoing sounds of heavy footsteps are rapidly approaching. Here we go again . . .

Rushing in, they lunge headlong as the big screw's monstrous weight crashes into my body. Tripping because of my shackles, I'm thrown to the floor and my back slams hard into the side of my steel cot. My forehead narrowly misses the bastard's jutting chin.

I wanted to make it look like an accident. Maybe next time.

Cuffs cut deeply into my pinned wrists, the shackles have bruised my ankles in the fall, my back is sore and . . . and . . . I can't breathe. I'm rolled onto my stomach and someone is pressing something hard against the back of my skull. It hurts like hell and it feels like a billy club. Face pressed against the cool floor . . . I can't see . . . the damn floor stinks of shit. Aided by a surge of burning fury and hatred, I manage to roll on my back. Looking up into their strained and sweaty faces, I spit a huge gob of phlegm into the prick's mouth. Eat THAT, screw.

The screw registers shock. He's incredulous. The skinny one with the twisted nose quickly grabs hold of my hair and pulls my head back. I can't feel any pain. They can't hit me, either—there are too many bodies in the line of fire. They couldn't hurt me anyway, the weak sluggards . . .

Uh oh, I'm being turned on my stomach again. We've been wrangling for a few minutes and I hear their heavy breathing.

The shackles are removed and the screws slowly pace backward and out into the corridor. My door slides shut with a loud clang, sealing out their ugly faces. They've left me cuffed, with only a mattress and the clothes on my back.

Struggling to my feet, I sit on the side of my cot

and feel the dull aching throb at the base of my skull. Parched lips and dried throat—I'm thirsty as hell, but I have no running water in my cell. It would be difficult to get a drink with these cuffs bound behind my back anyway. Wait, maybe the toilet water? I may have to slurp some up.

A stack of blue pages slide under my door. I know they're institutional charges. Probably a few for disobeying a direct order, using profane language, maybe some for threatening. This will make good toilet paper.

Hmmm . . . are they taking me to court again? I'm not going to move from this shithouse. I better rest and prepare for another assault.

5

Beaver Tail Justice

Sitting in this suffocating shaft. My hole in the wall. Society's parking lot, made expressly for the deviant. A testing ground. A human laboratory. Gladiator school. The Romans' infamous lions' den.

I wish the yellow-bellied low-life cowards would give me a shot at the title in a fair hand-to-hand combat. They wouldn't be disappointed; I can fight very well. In fact, is there anyone in this damnation den with a fifth-degree black belt or something? Bring him in . . .

The heavyset screw is muscular and he thinks he can fight. Assuming a boxing stance, this big bastard has thick arms and a barrel chest. No problem, watch this asshole. He's not just fighting a man with an athletic build. Oh, no, he's pitting himself in a duel against someone of unsurpassed madness and fury. My anger and hatred will cut right through him. I'll take him out and then finish the rest of them.

Bouncing lightly on his toes, the stooge looks in my eyes ... bad mistake. Placing my feet firmly, I jump quickly to his side and let go of a vicious left sidekick to his knee. It snaps like a twig. He screams in excruciating pain and his buddies are terrified. Spinning around, I square off with the others ... they remain motionless ... mouths agape ...

Elementary school, 1968

I'm a grade 4, sixty-pound kid and the burly teacher's shadow casts a dark cloud of doom over my diminutive figure. Bellowing, he orders me to remove my denim jacket and head to his office. From the look on his menacing face, I know I'm in serious trouble.

Taking giant strides, his heavy footsteps echo in the recesses of my spine. I'm shaking uncontrollably and dare not look at him. He looks so mean and ... so angry. Am I guilty of anything? I wonder where the other guy is. Why am I the only one who has to visit this ill-tempered monster? The other kid hit me first.

I've heard about the "visits" to this office. Rumors abound about the Sermon on the Mount, followed by loud cracks of thunder. These thoughts make me shudder as nervousness cramps my stomach. I feel queasy and the palms of my hands start to sweat. The last thing I want are sweaty palms when I might be getting the beaver tail treatment. I know that heavy rubber whip has caused much better boys to break down.

Tossing my jacket into my locker, I drag myself over to the dreaded office. As I sit waiting, a thought crosses my mind. I've heard that if I place a hair in the palm of my hand, the force of the blow from the whip could split my hand open and cause it to bleed. Yes, that will surely fix him and his whipping mentality. I pull a strand of hair from my head and carefully place it on the center line of my quivering palm.

The teacher takes the dreaded beaver tail from his desk.

Clutching the single strand of my hair in a death grip, I slowly extend my small hand. I stand face to belly with this militant authoritarian. Perspiration trickles down his bulging jowls as he methodically rolls up his sleeves.

Smelling his sweat mix with his medicinal aftershave, I begin to feel moisture forming in the palms of my quivering hands. I stand holding my breath, waiting for the assault to begin.

With a quick sweep of his giant paw, he brushes the hair away from my trembling hand. My duplicity is discovered. I'm caught. The teacher bellows as his thick lips contort in anger.

He raises his tree-trunk arm high over his head.

Time seems temporarily suspended. The silence in the confining cavern is deafening. The slim rubber strap is so small in his giant paw.

The strap begins to descend at such an incredible speed, I swear I hear molecules and atoms cracking in the gust of wind. Instinctively, I move my hand.

Whack . . . he mistakenly strikes himself in the groin with such force I feel hot air gushing from his mouth. The rush of wind brushes across my face as his thick neck muscles stiffens. Are those horns growing out of his head? His arms are as thick as trees. His massive head is affixed to his gargantuan frame with thick cables. Straightening his back, he composes himself . . . before I know it.

Crack . . . my stomach in knots, my mind racing, the sting penetrates to my spine. The wave of hot pain rushes through my shaking body. My knees are weak . . .

Sweat forming on my creased forehead, I wonder what the next blow will be like.

Crack . . . the second strike sends bolts of shock to my toes. Wincing, in excruciating pain, I can't comprehend the savagery. The palm of my hand is stinging as my head swims.

Crack . . . my hand is numb . . . I can't hold back any longer as tears flow freely down the length of my cheeks.

I try to compose myself before entering the class-full of friends, but to no avail. My friends peer at me curiously and I'm sure they can see my teary eyes. The heat of shame competes with my burning hands. Sitting at my desk, I place my trembling, stinging hands on the cool metal under my desk and let it soothe the heat emanating from my palms . . .

6

Roger Dodger

These violent and sordid imaginings. Why do they happen when I least expect it? Why am I spiraling down like this? Time . . . so much time with nothing to do. The mind has its limits . . . strong, but subject to whim. It goes off on its own to exact revenge.

And why should I want to stay here? It's natural to want to wander off. This is a nightmare and I promenade into dreams . . . but awful . . . so damned awful. I can almost taste the blood and guts. How can I reverse this?

I can stop, look and listen to my immediate surroundings, but I see and hear nothing. Bland walls, insane puppet masters, psychos and a mentality befitting henchmen. Barbarians. Absolute madmen. A small concrete cubicle with a steel bed, toilet and sink. No books, no music . . . the smells . . . rotten, putrid . . . nauseating shithouse.

Perhaps I can escape this world of chaos, mayhem and violence in sleep.

All right, then, how the hell am I going to sleep with these damned cuffs? I've done this a million times before. Pulling part of my black and white striped mattress up onto the wall, I've made myself an instant pillow. Leaving the other end on my cot, I stretch my weary body sideways and close my eyes. Now sleep, Ritchy . . . just drift, big guy . . . the wonder of escape in the dream world will come. No crickets, no noise. Feeling myself slipping into this blissful state . . . my only respite . . .

Elementary school, 1969
Big brown eyes sparkling with excitement, Roger strides innocently into my locker with blind loyalty. What an idiot. Roger Dodger barely tops four feet six inches. Perfect fit. He looks a bit cramped in my locker, but so would I.

Regarding me curiously, he's unsure of what's happening. Is he having second thoughts? I better act fast, because he may chicken out. Smiling broadly, I slowly close the blue metal door and lock it.

Roger begins to protest mildly, but I urge him in a hushed tone to keep silent as teachers pass by. Duped, my captive remains quiet and I slide surreptitiously into the classroom. Seated comfortably behind my desk I wait for the teacher to begin. See ya later, Roger Dodger.

I'm sitting smugly in class, when the teacher is interrupted by light muffled sounds that seem to be coming from somewhere outside. They're barely audible. I picture little Roger as his chest creeps with panic. I want to burst out laughing, but I must contain myself. The sound ceases just as the teacher looks curiously around the classroom. With a look of faint amusement, she shakes her head and resumes her lesson.

Struggling to suppress the outburst of laughter that's swelling inside, I bow my head on my desk. Shoulders shaking, my stomach tightens as I fight laughing out loud.

More minutes elapse before the mysterious muffled sounds start again. Roger has decided to add light knocks this time. My prisoner is getting worried. Oh, well . . . too late to do anything now . . . I can't just get up and confess . . . I'd get killed.

Startled, the teacher ceases her lesson. Looking curiously around the packed classroom, she asks if we hear what she's hearing. I'm going to burst at the seams for sure now. The teacher has this stupid look pasted on her face. Little Roger has been in my locker for what, two, three minutes?

Before anyone responds, hysterical and ear-

piercing cries of panic, coupled with the reverbera-
tions of crashing metal, are heard throughout the
entire school. Little Roger is freaking. His blaring
pitch is alarming.

Stiffening with fear, the teacher tosses her chalk
on the floor and runs out of the classroom, followed
by legions of terror-stricken students. I'm close
behind my panicked peers as we collide with teachers and students from adjacent classrooms. A mask
of fear grips their faces. There's panic and chaos in
the school. Be quiet, Roger; try to keep quiet, for
God's sake.

Oh, no, the freaking principal is rushing headlong
from his office, speeding across the long narrow
corridor with concern written large on his face. Dear
God. Looking around at the havoc I've wreaked, I'm
becoming more than a little concerned myself. I
turn and look at my best friend, Robert, whose face
has turned a shade of pale . . .

Whoa . . . my heart is beating like ninety. What the
hell is going on? That fat ugly diddler in the next cell
has interrupted my sleep again. He's screaming blue
murder. What the hell is his problem? Wait until *he*
tries to sleep. I know when he goes under; he snores
like a jackhammer. The fanatical screws are ignoring
him. His voice shrieks and the pitch is frightening. I

could swear someone is killing him. Is he dreaming about his past too?

Hmmm . . . I wonder why none of my old friends ever write or visit me? I mean, not even a card. Nothing. We go back many years, we went through elementary and high school together, but they don't even acknowledge my life. I'm alive . . . breathing . . . thinking . . . feeling.

I wonder how they're doing? Married? With kids? University? Good jobs? They have to be doing better than I am. Perhaps they think they're better than I am?

I guess friendships are nothing more than transient bonds. Nothing more than an illusion. These idiots don't even have any class, and no thoughts except for themselves. They're lucky they don't ever come here. I would let them protect themselves with their limited devices. They'd get hurt. They'd never make it two minutes in here.

I miss them . . . I should've never abandoned them when other friends came along in the first place. They feel betrayed. I know that feeling now . . .

7

Olympic Knockout

The 300-pound diddler who's molested little girls finally mellows out. I'm not sure if he was having a nightmare or just letting out the murderous fury of his real-life nightmare. In any case, he's quiet for now.

I'm thirsty as hell. I wish I could take a drink of water, but I won't ask the man for any favors. I'd rather die than ask these demons for anything. A man can survive for three to four days without water anyway. If I need it, there's water in my toilet.

I was born in the wrong time. I'm out of place. I should have been born when humanity was more fully evolved. More mentally and emotionally mature, more aware . . . more damn humane.

I'm awake now, so what am I going to do for the next few hours? What time is it? Is it day or night? The place is quiet, so it must be . . . I don't have a clue. What does it matter anyway? Time is time is time and I'll be out in a few days and carry out my plan. Yes . . . the beautiful plan . . . I'll do it . . .

Welcome to my nightmare, you sons of bitches. That fat parole officer in the corner looks famished and weakened . . . what experiment should I conduct with you today? You seem to have lost a good fifty pounds. Talk about a great weight loss program. Would you recommend me to your friends? Tell me where your best friend lives or I kill the bitch right now.

He's horrified and defeated. I'm serious; I want to know where your best friend lives, and I want to know it right now. Address, telephone and vital statistics, like if your friend has a wife and whether they have some kids. Don't pretend to be moral and just, asshole. You want to play the hero? Bravado is always met with death. The martyr with a death wish . . .

These fantasies—they're becoming increasingly vivid and plentiful. I have too much dead time and not enough to do in this hole. No books, no radio, no nothing. When did I cross the line from fantasy to reality? When did I decide to do this for real? I know I'm nuts and I know I'll kill every one of these screws. Nobody can blame me for that, can they? I'm prepared to die for this noble cause. I was a pretty good kid once, but now my innocence has been raped and torn apart. I can't trace the exact point where my mind crossed over that fine line. Am I going insane? I must be. Some people would think so—but they haven't experienced this hellish dimension.

It's very hard to understand, but who wouldn't want to murder and mutilate after being subjected to such a brutal regime for so many years? I've heard of university students who have simulated lockup situations in something called the Stockholm experiment. These otherwise good kids ended up hating their peers who played the part of screws. Even though their lockup was only for a few hours, the students nonetheless spiraled into hatred and fury. Can they imagine and empathize with seven long years of these nightmare conditions?

These kids were not even close to the real thing. The simulation lacked ingredients of the grim reality. The screws weren't this brutal and the cons weren't this crazy, were they? I don't think so. Hypothetical situations can't compare to the genuine article. I don't think they beat each other, spit and pissed at one another, chained and shackled each other. I can't see them burning one another with mace and slamming one another with powerful fire hoses. The experiment was superficial. Yet they felt themselves spiraling.

What about serving 400 days in the hole? What about the vicious mentality around here? It's kill or be killed. The bluffs turn into the genuine article after a while. At what precise moment this occurs is still a mystery to me. Over any period, my condition deteriorates. Imperceptibly, slowly, over time I'm pushed over the edge. It's natural. Anybody would lose it, man. There's no escape and no respite from the constant torment. Nobody is doing anything about it, either.

I was a good kid once. I had everything going for me. I had a host of great friends and I was pursuing my dreams. How many thirteen-year-olds have a dream? I had it together for a long time. I was dedicated and worked hard . . .

Teenager, 1973

Twenty-one months into boxing training and I'm in peak shape to perform, fighting endlessly without tiring. My bout with the Canadian champion is set for next week and I have no doubt that I'll win.

I train for many hours on my own, away from the club. I sleep and eat with this championship in mind. I wake up thinking about it and fall asleep with visions of success. This fight will bring me one step closer to my dream of becoming an Olympic athlete.

One day, dissension breaks out at the club. Envy is leaving its putrid stench in our small clubroom. My peers are questioning why the junior fighter is facing the champ. They note that some of our club's more experienced fighters have fought the champ and failed—but why should I get the chance? They

figure I'm not as experienced and they want a
rematch first.

The sour grapes have forgotten that I'm the one
who's gone to Toronto and the States and defeated
opponents who'd decisively beat these so-called
more experienced fighters in our club. Aside from
their short memories, I feel hurt and betrayed by
their rumblings and wonder where the team spirit
has gone. Fortunately, not all the fighters in the club
think the same, but the feelings are strong enough
to leave their mark.

One night, the rumbling turns into clear chatter as
we're leaving the club. The primary source becomes
crystal-clear as I sit in a neighbor's car waiting for
the drive back home. One of this neighbor's kids
had lost to the champ a few months before. This boy
is two years older than me and had started to train
at the club a few months before I arrived. He
believes I could never beat the champ if he lost to
him. This crybaby estimates he's a far better fighter
than me.

I try to pacify the big suck by assuring him I don't
consider myself superior, but I believe I have a
chance on the strength of my style. My attempts do
little to quell the whining and I sense he wants to
take me on.

I am in the back seat of the car with the whiner's
little brother while the whiner barks at me from the

front seat. As the taunting persists, I begin to
wonder when his father will come out of the club. I
know where all this is going.

Now the little brother is siding with him, and I
find myself in the middle of a barrage of insults and
put-downs. I am feeling closed in. I'm getting
nervous and pumped.

The big brother throws the first punch. Twisting
his body, knees tight against the back of his seat, he
lets go with a solid right hand. I dodge and the blow
brushes my ear. I duck as I sense the younger
brother begin to shift his weight so he too can deliver.

I swing my right arm behind the younger brother
and fling him to the floor, where he is stuck between
the back and front seats. Sliding off the back seat, I
pin him and rain punches into his surprised face.
The kid panics and tries to raise his hands in front
of his face. I land five to seven blows to his face and
head as blood spews everywhere. The older brother
is hammering away at the back of my head, but his
blows have little effect. I'm just so pumped.

The little brother done and finished, I swing
around and give the elder some attention in return.
Grabbing a handful of his reddish hair with one
hand, I tug on his plaid shirt with the other. Pulled
over the seat, he joins his bleeding brother between
the seats.

Their freckled faces are splattered with blood and

I can't fathom what are freckles, what's blood. It's getting very messy.

Squeezing out the back door of the car, I manage to take a few steps before the older brother jumps me. We're turning and twisting on the mud-soaked ground when his father bellows.

That scuffle costs me everything I had trained so hard for in the two years before. My chance to fight the Canadian champion and to head to the Olympics vanish at that very moment. I'm left holding thin air. What a technical knockout . . .

Talk about a king knockout. I'm going to knock you out and take you down for keeps. That's how we do things here in the Haven. I have only a few days to go, asshole. I may be cuffed right now, but I have a set of cuffs for you too. Cuffs at the side of the head, jerkoff . . .

Files are strewn across the desk, my prisoner is gagged and tied. The parole rep has some paperwork on Willy. Look at what they have inscribed within. No wonder we always get labeled and stereotyped. Self-proclaimed shrinks . . . they have no idea what they're talking about . . . the joint has no part in this chaos? Self-defeating patterns . . . volatile personality . . . multiple personality disorder. . . . Look at yourselves. Everyone has a dual personality. Look, you're a two-

face. Your actions belie the morals you seek to instill and impart ... you can't transmit what you lack ... you're not a role model. Show us something different from what we already know.

His partially unbuttoned white shirt reveals war tattoos. He may be a veteran of the Second World War ... how do you like the third?

8

Big Jean

The crickets. Oh, no, not those annoying, mind-breaking crickets again. It must be late evening. I can't take another night of this torture. I'm going to snap for certain. QUIET! They won't stop. They echo in my vent for hours and never stop. My dungeon provides perfect acoustics for their racket. GAAAD, I hate this hellhole.

The sounds are like crashing cymbals by now. How long will they go on tonight? I'll have to get busy to avoid going crazy. I will stir up some shit and get the administration to act on this bullshit. What am I going to do? I'm still cuffed, but I have the use of my feet. I know . . . I can kill two birds with one stone. I'll lie on my back and kick my steel door until the screws come and fight with me. We'll get it on and that fat diddler in the next cell will be forced to hear my sounds of music. The night shift is not going to get any rest tonight either. I'll drive them all nuts along with me.

KABOOM ... the first blow sends a shattering, ear-popping crash reverberating through the bowels of the hole. I'm certain the guys in segregation next door can hear me. Must hit harder and let the guys in population hear my fury as well.

KABOOM ... this blow echoes loudly and chases the first down the narrow labyrinth of this hellish hole. My mind is shut and I'm only focused on my footing. No shackles this time and the movement is great.

I bang endlessly and the tempo picks up. I close my eyes and let my feet slam into the cold hard steel of my door. The numbness is coming. Good ... KABOOM ... KABOOM ... KABOOM ... KABOOM...

Well, well, well, look at what just peered into my cell. It's the stupid screw with the blue eyes and crooked nose. What's the matter, asshole? Can't sleep? Can't earn your twenty dollars an hour sitting on your fat ass at my expense? Let me give you something to work for. Come in my cave and try to stop me, asshole.

The bastard has a sneer on his face. The mindless bastard ... this is nothing ... wait till he visits *my* prison. He'll bang and bang, but I'll kick his face in ...

Teenager, 1974

In phase two of my karate training, Big Jean decides
the time is ripe for me to experience another
dimension of the fight game. Theory is over and
practical schooling is about to begin. Big Jean
selects a rock 'n' roll tavern on the outskirts of town
as our field of experimentation. I'm only fifteen
years old, five foot four tall and weigh in at 120.
That doesn't deter Big Jean. After all, who is going
to challenge HIM to see my ID at the door? The guy
is five-ten, weighs 220, has muscles from head to
foot and hits like a ton of lead if punked off.

Jumping into his customized van, Big Jean and I
drive the five miles out of town and arrive at the
preferred destination. The drive has been unusually
quiet. As we pull into the large parking lot packed
with cars and trucks and step out of his light blue
van, we're welcomed by the sounds of heavy metal
flowing through the crisp night air.

As I saunter nervously beside Big Jean into the
bar, the overpowering smell of stale draft and cigarette smoke attaches itself to my clothing. I'm
feeling very anxious as I follow Big Jean to the area
around the pool table, where the smoke forms a pall
of blue mist around the boisterous patrons. Sitting
at a small wooden table, I'm overwhelmed by the
beehive of activity and assaulted by music.

A waitress with super-tight blue denim jeans and

a scanty pink halter top takes Jean's order and brings back two extra-tall bottles of beer. As she leans over our table, her breasts are inches from spilling out of her top. Her blond hair is tied back behind sunken features; blue mascara gives her a hardened appearance.

Scanning the intimidating stature of Big Jean, I note that his shoulders have burst the seams of his short-sleeved tank top. Despite this security, I can't get comfortable in this strange scene. I've never gone to a bar. People seem so disjointed . . . disoriented and unaware.

Sipping his beer, Big Jean tells me to observe my environment. He talks in a high-pitched tone. I can barely hear what he's saying above the heavy metal blasting from the speakers. He wants me to make mental notes of several people and their habits. I'm asked to monitor the liquor flow of about ten drinkers in my direct vicinity and observe their temperaments. I have to know if they smoke and what brand, how many beers they've been drinking and if they drink from glasses. Are their ashtrays full, color of their pants, their company, who they talk to, their language, etc.

Leaning closer toward me, Big Jean makes me aware of the three exits in our view and states smartly that we should always keep our backs to the wall.

I'm very aware of the three rednecks seated beside our table who are not only drinking their tall bottles of beer like they're ginger ale, but are also being humiliated at the pool table. The heavyset guy beside me is so close I can feel the heat of his shoulder on mine. Big Jean doesn't have to suggest keeping an eye on these monsters. They look like they just came out of the woods, for God's sake. They're big—bigger than Jean himself—and very profane.

Scanning the many faces in my new surroundings, some drinking, others smoking, I feel an uneasiness stirring in the pit of my stomach. I note that some of the prettiest women drink just as much as the big rednecks.

As the night progresses and my homework persists, Jean leans over the table and, whispering in my ear, tells me to pay closer attention to my neighbor's bottle of beer. What?

I'm getting very scared now. What could this mean? What the hell is happening here? What kind of place is this? I can't imagine anyone wanting to hit a kid in the face with a beer bottle. Nobody is that crazy, are they? I haven't done anything or said a word to anyone.

Suddenly, the redneck beside me picks up his bottle and raises it in the air. Fear grips my stomach as I instinctively duck as quickly as I can. I put my hands over my head, my face hugs my knees. My heart is racing; I'm paralyzed by fright.

Doubled up with my cheeks to my knees, I see Big Jean's feet stride quickly across my field of vision and stop directly in front of my bottle-swinging neighbor. Big Jean's extremely fast.

Jean knocks the bottle out of the redneck's hand. Shards of broken glass bounce off the wall and fly in every direction. I think, this guy almost disfigured me for life.

I can feel the beer spray down my back as Big Jean delivers a vicious punch. I hear the impact of the guy's head as it slams into the wall. He falls headlong at Jean's feet, face down, eyes sealed tight.

Straightening myself, I press my back against the wall, feeling the wetness of my Van Halen T-shirt. I don't dare get in the way. I don't want to get hit accidentally by one of Big Jean's powerful blows.

Before the next redneck can react, Big Jean delivers a lightning-quick right cross to his bearded chin. Blood sprays in the air and splashes on neighboring tables. That blow sends the redneck reeling to the floor. I'm sure his jaw is shattered.

These two are out cold. I've never seen anybody knocked out. Everything is moving in fast-time. This is scaring the shit out of me. Maybe these guys are crippled. Or dead. My heart is beating madly and I wonder what will happen next.

The third redneck, who has his back to Big Jean, is half-turned in his seat. A burly fellow, he grimaces and snarls as he gets a grip on Big Jean's shirt and tries to pull himself up. Big Jean shoots his hand out powerfully and palms the guy so hard and fast, I doubt he knows what hit him. Blood splatters all over his face as he buckles to the floor. His nose must be pushed to his brain. Is he dead? . . .

A cross-eyed screw comes to my door. He has company. Are they going to entertain me again? The food slot creaks open and I see the end of the mace gun.

What's the matter with these screws? They don't like my banging or what? They shouldn't have thrown me in the hole in the first place. What business is it of theirs how I survive here? I had to pummel that kid. He would have gotten me killed for ignoring the prison codes. I never hurt him that bad. He can go on living his pitiful life . . .

9

High School Daze

A thin stream squirts through my food slot. I try to turn my face away, but I'm too slow. The spray hits my face just below my chin and trickles down my chest. The burning sensation will start soon; it will feel like layers of skin are being burned off my body.

Then the door of my cell opens wide and the sound of heavy boots echoes off my dull walls . . . this fat screw . . . the bulging jowls . . . short-cropped hair . . . sleazebag . . . he reminds me of a teacher in high school . . .

Stoner/Fighter, 1975
The teacher with the thick black mane and wide shoulders makes a hapless target for one of Dan's paperclips. Whizzing through the air at incredible speed, the clip smacks the teacher in the middle of his back. Seated behind me in class, Dan chokes back his laughter. Stoned from smoking a joint

during lunch break, I bow my head over my desk and chuckle silently . . .

A few seconds elapse before I sense the teacher looming beside me. Head crooked in the fold of my elbow, I look slightly down to my left and see his polished, size 13 shoes at my side. Uh, oh . . .

Suddenly, a hard blow slams into the base of my skull and my nose hits the desk. Tears begin to swell in my hazy eyes. I see red . . .

Lifting my head slowly, I shake my head and clear my befogged brain while I wipe the tears from my eyes. Everything is hazy and distanced. I can't see a damn thing. The back of my head is throbbing, for God sakes. What kind of animal is this?

My hand scans the smooth cool surface of my desk, searching madly for my pencils and pens. I wonder if I'm bleeding on my desk. Could it be blood? Pumped, I seize a handful of pencils and pens and stand face to face with the madman.

The classroom is silent. Everyone is shocked. I can't see anything or hear a word. All I want to do is drive something into his big belly. My mind racing, my hands tighten on the pencils and pens. I imagine piercing his bulging guts under his crisp white shirt. Lead poisoning for you, you big piece of shit.

Wiping the last of the tears from my face, I burn my eyes into his and tell him to go fuck himself. I want him to respond and react. Anything will do.

Any provocation will cause his guts to be filled with lead and ink. The bastard says nothing. He just stands in front of me, speechless.

I should kick him in the bag. He'd double over and I'd drive the pens into his back.

Incensed, I throw them on the floor, call him a big pig and storm out of the classroom . . .

Lying on my back, I struggle to get to my feet. I'm in a terrible position. Before I can make it up, the whole battery crashes heavily atop my sprawled body. Knees slam into my stomach and chest and arms seize every opening they can. Arms twisting, legs seized, one screw has his shoes on my hair. I'm caught, immobile. It's like fighting an octopus. Tentacles sucking at me . . . trying to take my blood and my spirit.

What? Is this goon with thin lips and a scar on his cheek going to punch me? He looks very pissed off. Those black curly locks . . . dark complexion . . .

Stoner/Fighter, 1975

On a cold winter afternoon, Big Jean and I stride to the gym for a look around. Still cold from our jaunt on snow-covered sidewalks, Jean and I take note of Mark standing by the trampoline watching Linda perform her routine as we enter the gym.

Mark is encouraging her to work hard, smiling broadly, and Linda is delighted with the attention. As she jumps, Linda's supple long black curly hair falls lightly over beautiful features and her blue eyes sparkle with enthusiasm.

My heart leaps. She always looks so terrific and today is no exception. My little Linda is built like Wonder Woman, but she's so sweet and innocent. She's twirling and turning like a real pro. I can envision her in the Olympics.

Big Jean never misses a beat. He's quick to stir up feelings of jealousy. Seeing my face tinge with red, Big Jean begins telling me that Mark is disrespectful to me and wants Linda. He has me going nuts in no time. With Big Jean encouraging me, I stride over to Mark.

The urge to hit Mark is overpowering. My muscles tense up and my mind visualizes my attack. Oblivious to me, Mark is resting his arms and hands on the blue steel railing of the trampoline. His body hunched forward, he continues to pump Linda up. I'm becoming more jealous with every passing moment.

I grab a thick handful of his black hair and slam his forehead into the steel railing. The force and the sound of the blow stop Linda abruptly as she stands in shock and terror . . .

The monstrosity gets up and leaves my cell as the others slip my cuffs off and retreat from my dungeon. Watching the goon squad slink out of my hole, an unshakable conviction seizes me. This whole ordeal is nothing but one big stupid game. All they want to do is use me as their test subject. They want to provoke and antagonize me to practise their tactics for creating submission and to beat the boredom.

Holy shit, the sting from the mace gun is starting to burn. I swear blisters are going to bubble up on my chest and my neck. My skin, it's beet red . . . this is intolerable.

Hunched over my toilet bowl, I cup my hands and, scooping up the cool water, splash it on my burning body. It brings very little relief.

The damn toilet water stinks. I need warm water, but I have none in here. My sink is disabled because I flooded my cell a few days ago. This thing is not over. The mace is penetrating my pores . . . it's running through me like fire . . . my nasal passages are burning and my eyes are blinded.

Lying flat on my stomach on the cool cement floor . . . this might help . . . it's not . . . the blistering heat is unbearable . . .

10

Crossing Over

The searing heat of mace has subsided, but the sting lingered for a long time. I just lay on the cold concrete floor until shivers swallowed me whole. Why did they have to mace me anyway? The assholes like to hurt people. They're vindictive and hurtful bastards. They hate me. That screw with Bugs Bunny buckteeth and cross-eyes didn't have the jam to hit me. He couldn't hurt me anyway. But if I let him have one of mine . . . he'd break like a papier-mâché doll . . .

Let them play their stupid games; I'll be out very soon anyway. For now, I better get myself in tip-top shape before I take them out and erase them from the face of the earth.

Stretch, big fella, stretch those hams. Straining . . . blood rushing to my head . . . have to touch my forehead to my knees while keeping my legs straight. Come on . . . I used to be able to touch my head to my knees while standing ... almost there ... close ... good, there it is.

All right now, hit the floor and one, two, three, four ... thirty ... forty ... fifty ... straining ... sixty ... up ... it's burning ... go for seventy, kid ... all right. Not bad; I can still crank off seventy clean and full pushups. Wow, the chest is pumped big-time. Flexing, I recall how I could once place a cup of coffee on my pectorals while sitting. Slabs of muscle fold over my chest like beefsteaks. Have to loosen up before the bozos come back for another round of their mindless games.

Okay, throw a few combinations. Snapping left jab to the nose, tears flowing, blinding my opponent. Duck quickly and smash the right cross to the ribs and he doubles over. Straightening, I finish him off with a solid left hook to the jaw. That combo knocked out a few jerks in my day. Maybe I can kill someone if I smash them in the temple. Maybe drive the bridge of their nose into their brain. I've taken out a few jerks with this deadly combo. They flew across the floor and slammed helplessly into furniture and walls.

I'm loosening up very nicely now. Nice and limber with a good snap at the end. I must never go down, never go unconscious, no matter what happens or how badly I'm hurt. These guys can—and do—kill.

You never know what they'll do once they have you down. They might not stop. They're bloodthirsty psychos. At least I'll give them an opportunity to speak when I knock them down.

They found one con beheaded. His head was in his toilet bowl . . .

Stoner/Fighter, 1976

Fighting, drinking, drugging, womanizing, driving around day and night, delivering drugs and hitting the local hotels is the norm for us. We drive around in Al's customized Ford pickup with all the trimmings. Side pipes bellowing, powerful engine roaring, my head popped out of the sunroof, we squeal the mag tires around every corner in town. Once we've picked up our dope supply, we guzzle gin and go all over town to sell acid, hash, oil and pot.

Life for Al and me is one big drunk. The parties we attend verge on insanity. Cases upon cases of beer fill the refrigerators and porches, while people sneak around frantically trying to stash their liquor supply for the morning after. Brutal fights break out at the slightest provocation. How many people have I hammered to the ground? Thirty? Forty? Fifty?

I love to test a person's conviction and might. They like to think they're big . . . I hit first and talk later. I've seen what sucker punches can do and I know from experience that delivering the first blow increases the chance of victory tenfold. I always hit first. I can take a good walloping and deliver some good ones in return . . .

One seventy-five, seventy-six, seventy-seven. Come on, kid, you can do at least 200 more. Even 500 situps isn't that much. The gut is rippled and nobody can hit hard enough to double me over. Big Mike can stand on the bench press, hold a medicine ball high over his head and slam it on my stomach and I don't even flinch.

I've worked up a pretty good sweat now: 400 pushups, 500 situps, countless leg raises, seven to eight rounds of kickboxing, excellent stretches, free-standing squats, and what else did I do?

Can I remember some of my words? Vacuous, vapid, perspicacity, percipience, acumen, shibboleth, vitriolic, eschew, obfuscation, diatribe, sentinel, maudlin, apex, epitome, vex, stentorian. I've added several thousand words to my vocabulary. I've studied numerous vocabulary-building books along with the dictionary.

I've written some damn good grievances while I've been in here. The administration was stumped on the first paragraph. Stupid jerks.

I always enjoyed words at school, and athletics too. It's served me well. Was it all preparation?

WOW ... I wonder if fate and destiny had this in mind all along? Both my fighting skills and my word power have come in handy around here. The words for the screws and the fists for the cons ...

Stoner/Fighter, 1976

I enjoy wrestling at school and I've got great potential. Unfortunately, the favored champ gets jealous and the matter comes to a head when he and his friends confront me on a sunny summer day, while I'm waiting for the bus to take me home from high school.

Long blond curls tied loosely at the back of his big head, his chest pumped up and muscular arms swaying at his sides, he stops in front of me and, sneering, asks if I think I'm tough.

His faded blue denim jeans are torn at the knees, his blue and red plaid shirt is partly unbuttoned. He is obviously very strong and looks like a seasoned street fighter. His high cheekbones and clear blue eyes remind me of the Russian fighter in Bruce Lee's *Fist of Fury*. He has to weigh at least 150 pounds against my 120.

With knotted features and twisted mouth, he approaches within foot-striking distance. As he shuffles nearer, his friends begin to chant and encourage him to beat the living shit out of me.

I feel the crowd beginning to spread and form a human circle that will form our duelling den.

As always in these situations, the crowd vanishes from my mind's eye and everything happens in a death-like silence. All my senses are piqued and supersensitive. I can even smell his cheap after-shave and medicinal deodorant.

His eyes, they're so eager, and his body tense. His arrogant head thrown proudly back, he clenches his rock-hard fists.

He makes the cardinal mistake. Telegraphing is a sign of an inexperienced fighter and this guy can be read for miles. He shifts his weight back for a moment, then lunges forward to put me in a vise-like headlock. His arms swish through air as I duck and wrap my arm around his waist, lift him slightly off his feet and turn quickly, slamming him to the ground. Keeping my arm around his waist, I roll on the ground and onto his heaving chest.

Sitting comfortably atop his stretched body, I look intently into his surprised face. He looks up at me with such a stupid grin I almost feel sorry for the idiot. I want to slam my fist into his face, but I'm afraid of what I'll do to it. What if I break his cheekbone or shatter his pearly white teeth? He didn't even hurt me and I'm not angry. Give me a reason to get pumped and you'll have to deal with my wrath.

Releasing my grip, I stand and pace away to give him a choice to either back out of this fight or spark it up again. He walks over to his friends, who appear to be very disappointed with his effort. He tells them I'm lucky and it's not over. Yeah, right.

The long yellow bus rolls to a stop and we clamber onboard. Grabbing a seat at the back of the bus, I position my back to the window as the group follows close behind.

Seated comfortably, still a little jittery from the fight, I watch him. His face is taut with frustration. Curling his upper lip, the idiot starts provoking me again. Standing in front of me, with his friends behind him, he's telling me he's going to get off at my stop and show me how to finish a fight for good. Butterflies start to dance in my stomach. I've no desire to have my nose broken or eyes blackened. Did I make a mistake when I let him get up?

I decide to capitalize on the element of surprise. I jump quickly to my feet, grab hold of the overhead steel bar with both hands and let the bottoms of my feet slam into his chest.

He reacts too late. Face contorted, his flailing forearms cutting through the wind, both his feet leave the ground. He crashes heavily into the steel-slatted seats on the opposite side. Looking down on his slumped body, I know he won't get up and try anything more . . .

Not again. My food slot opens wide and the screw wants me to read something. What the hell are they up to now? The thin screw with the crossed eyes has a smirk on his face and I know this is just another stupid head game.

Unfolding the sheet of paper, I discover that the stupid warden has me on a strict sandwich and water diet because I've thrown my food and hot coffee at the walls and the screws before this. To add insult to injury, the jerk wants me to write him a letter requesting regular meals.

11

Crash Test Dummy

Watching the skinny screw walk away, I demand he bring a pencil and paper like the good slave he is. "Make it fast, asshole." What a bunch of idiots. Do they think I'll write a letter to the stupid warden? Maybe I'll compose such a powerful letter to the idiot, he'll need an English professor to translate it. He and his cronies are not that bright to begin with.

I can put my vocabulary-building exercises into practice with these numbskulls. I'll show them who the doorknob is around here. They have no idea who they're playing with. I'm not some half-wit mental case wasting away in this hole. I'm a lot smarter than any of these fools.

Haven't I read some of the greatest philosophers and free thinkers of the world? I think, therefore I am. What doesn't kill me makes me stronger. As a self-taught person, I know a thing or two. Reading is my greatest pastime around this mind-numbing joint, when I'm not in this damned stinkhole.

These screws would be lucky if they understood what the hell I say, never mind Descartes, Nietzsche, Shakespeare, Tacitus, Aristotle, Plato, St. Augustine, Rousseau, Voltaire, Diderot, Euclid, Aquinas and all the other great writers, critical thinkers and classic and historical novelists.

Wouldn't Thomas Paine have something to say about this society? I know Edmund Burke would buy into it, the white-buttoned snotbag. Dostoyevsky and Hugo experienced this kind of totalitarian regime. Political prisoners of the past, these great men understand the mystification of social justice.

I may not be as well-read as some people, but I can still read, write and understand. Oh, yes, I understand.

This stupid little food game is just another attempt to break me. Child's play. This kind of punishment—head game, power trip, and control—can never break me. My beliefs are beyond their psychological warfare.

Damn them. My resolve to resist is strengthened by their efforts to break me. I'm resilient. To hell with their Mickey Mouse head games . . .

Joy Ride, 1976
Ron and I decide we'll skip school and head to his friend's. Short, blond and blue-eyed, Ron comes

from what my buddies call snob hill, but with Ron and me, these petty social distinctions mean little. We share a party hearty attitude. Sex and drugs and rock 'n' roll.

Sauntering under the hot sun for a few short blocks, we arrive at an apartment building I've been to before. In fact, I've done chinups on the side railing of my ex-girlfriend's eighth floor balcony. Stoned.

We take the elevator up a few floors, then stroll through the carpeted hallway to a dark wooden door, where we knock before being let into a small apartment.

A half-dozen teenage boys are huddled closely together in a dimly lit room filled with smoke and the smell of pot. Smoke drifts into the hallway as we open the door and spills its blue pall through the balcony door at the other end of the room.

I recognize a few of the kids by face and some by name. They've pulled the sectional sofas and kitchen chairs into a circle in the living room and are passing each other huge joints and large tumblers of drinks. Their stool-pigeon eyes easily give them away. It's obvious these guys are very stoned.

I pull my eyes away from this bizarre scene and glance at the other end of the living room, where I see an overstocked bar overflowing with a vast array of bottles.

Rows of bottles are lined up inside the small
hutch and stand atop its smooth surface like turrets
on a castle. I can't even begin to identify the many
brands. There are tall, slim-necked bottles, short fat
jugs, dark- and light-colored liquids—the works.
This is a party room if I've ever seen one.

Uneasiness stirs in the pit of my gut as Ron
motions me toward the center of the cramped living
room. I slump on a plush sofa beside some guy
who's completely boiled. His eyes are flaming red.
His curly brown hair is haggard and unkempt, yet
his clothes look expensive.

Four joints are sparked in unison, as if on cue, on
my arrival. At the same time, large tumblers of a
whiskey, gin and rye mixture pass from hand to
shaky hand.

A big fat joint comes in my direction and I hesitate. All eyes fall upon me. I'm very uncomfortable,
and beginning to think of this scene as some form of
ritualistic suicide.

Their eyes remain fixed on me . . .

Picking up the jumbo joint from my neighbor, I
inhale the bitter smoke, and as soon as I release it,
another arrives. The liquor is being passed along in
a similar manner and I can't decide which to take
and which to leave, so I do like everyone else and
take both simultaneously. A joint in one hand and a
drink in another, I inhale the thick blue smoke, hold

it in my lungs and ingest a mouthful of whatever happens to be in my hand before I exhale thick clouds of smoke.

The preppy seated next to me blows thick streams of smoke from the end of his joint into my lungs. These shotguns have a dizzying impact. Some of the joints are made of a combination of hash, grass and oil, and after about an hour of this madness, the rum, rye, vodka and gin mixtures start tasting like fruit punch.

In a very short time, I too am completely fried. I vaguely recall leaving the apartment and have hazy recollections of kicking and breaking the windows in the front door of the lobby on my way out of the building. The next thing I remember is standing in the hot sun, swaying dizzily by a curb a block away from Ron's home.

Numbed and disoriented, I see Ron's attention is focused on a group of people chatting on a front veranda. Looking closer, I realize Ron is not at all interested in the people, but rather their brand-new automobile. The shiny red Mustang is idling quietly as the midday sun reflects off its tinted glass.

Turning swiftly toward me with a grimace on his drunken face, Ron suggests we take the car for a ride. Swaying dizzily, I look into Ron's glossy eyes and laugh heartily. What a joker, I think to myself. But he doesn't seem to be kidding. Coaxing and cajoling, he tries to talk me into walking toward the car.

I figure he'll back away once we get close to the vehicle, so to entertain his playfulness, I stagger along beside him. As we wobble along, I stop and look at Ron. To my astonishment, he still looks serious.

Standing hesitantly by the car, I pull my eyes away from him and look over at the people on the veranda one last time. Chatting merrily, they're not paying any attention to us.

At this point, Ron starts daring me to hop into the driver's side. He's relentless—pumping me up and daring me. I decide at that very moment to take his prank further. I'll turn the joke around and scare him a bit, but I'm certainly not going to steal the car. I'll get into the car, but that's as far as I'll go.

I swing the door open and slide into the driver's seat. I let my body sink comfortably into the leather seat.

The sound of people screaming yanks me out of my reverie. The people on the veranda are gesturing frantically and a stout gray-haired fella is rushing toward the vehicle like a rhinoceros. Wow, I'm only kiddin', man.

Ron's yelling at me to move out. My mind is racing. Everything's in a haze. I can't believe I'm in the car. Ron is frantic and yells louder as more people start running toward us. I slam my foot on the accelerator, the engine roars fiercely, but we remain motionless. I'm panicking.

Ron tells me to put the car in gear. I can't. I'm frozen in fright. The people are approaching the vehicle fast and the old fart almost has his hand on the doorhandle.

Reaching over, Ron slams the shift into gear. Suddenly, the car lurches forward as squealing tires send gravel flying in every direction. The car is out of control before we've gone ten feet.

Good God! Focusing through a blur, I see that we're closing in on a ninety-degree corner at incredible speed. I know that I'm not going to make it. This beast is already traveling at over fifty miles an hour. Tires squealing, the car swerves around the corner.

The car begins to fishtail. I'm scared people might be on the street. Can't stop. I'm confused and trying to see through a blur . . . everything is moving too fast. A cement hydro pole looms at close range. I freeze for a second.

Then I slam my foot on the accelerator. The pedal is to the metal—the car's speeding up, weaving and careening. Then we crash.

The impact is vicious. My chest smashes into the steering wheel with such force I believe my sternum is broken. There's not an ounce of breath left in my

lungs as my head slams violently into the windshield and my limp body reels backward like a crash
test dummy.

Everything blurs. Is Ron exhorting me to run? His
little hands tug on my tired arms, grabbing, pulling,
but I'm not sure. I think I hear him pleading with
me to snap out of my daze and escape. His voice is
distant and his words trail off. I can taste blood . . .
want to sleep . . . don't care anymore.

My legs are caught under the dash. I can't move
them. Peering through a haze, I see what appears to
be the engine resting above my knees. Are my legs
broken?

Can't straighten at all. My head's being pushed
forward and I can't move. The roof of the car is
pressed against my head. Through the shattered
windshield, I see the hydro pole on top of the car.
I'm suffocating.

I'm cramped and I'm stuck, and shattered glass
from the windshield sticks to my arm and my forehead like stucco. Brushing my face with a trembling
hand, I pull away a handful of blood and glass.

Dizzy, confused, and semiconscious, I can't focus.
My head is swimming and my heart palpitating. I'm
going under . . . under . . .

12

Sentenced

Time is time is time. I pass from moment to moment without point of reference.

What was John Howard thinking? The Quakers— real quacks. I feel no inner peace. I have nothing but hatred and fury as companions.

Penitence and punishment are irreconcilable. They can never bring about change because one destroys the other. We who are inside are stripped of all sensibilities. The killers, recidivism and violent crimes prove the system is failing. Christ, my own mental state speaks volumes about your barbaric practices . . .

Book 'em, Danno, 1976
I awake to Al's face behind bars. Shaking the cobwebs from my mind, I look about the . . . the empty cell. N O O O O O . . .

It hits me like a bolt of lightning. The damn accident. I'm in jail. I'm in a filthy prison.

My friend is not saying anything. This could never have happened to me, yet here I am, trapped and caged like some animal. But this can't be happening.

How could I have been so stupid? Can't believe this . . . what did I do? The damn hydro pole . . . where's Ron?

The smells and sounds of this place are like nothing I could have imagined. Hard steel bars surround me. A stink lingers in the air and mixes with antiseptic cleansers.

These bars, they pierce through my skin and shoot into my spine, leaving me cold and shivering. I'll vomit . . . my head is swimming . . .

I'm nothing but an extension of this steel cage and empty void. The place . . . it reverberates into nothingness . . .

The silence . . . it's deafening. It envelops my very being from head to toe. The cold . . . the deafening silence . . .

Al and I are already worlds apart, yet he is no more than a foot away. The steel bars separate our existences. We're divided physically, spiritually, emotionally and mentally. I'm now a crook and a felon. I screwed up. I can read the pain in my friend's face, but what can I say?

Looking intently into my eyes, Al asks, "What the fuck happened, Rick?"

"Shit, man, I don't know, Al. The fucking car just went out of control." I'm trying to ignore the pounding in my head and I feel like vomiting. The damn cell is spinning.

Sighing heavily, Al looks around the empty cell and shakes his head in despair.

Anxiety twists my guts as I struggle to recall the events. But all I draw is a blank.

"The car just flew out of control," is all I could repeat, like some bad mantra.

I begin to think about all the good times Al and I have had together. We loved our freedom and partying. Every day was a holiday with lots of things to do. We had plenty of cash and always enjoyed lots of action. Al was always generous and treated me like a brother. I lived at his house and we did everything together. I thought of him as a brother too.

I remember the time Al and I drove to Toronto wired on California acid. Doug and Pablo came along and I almost killed myself on the 401. I jumped from the back of Al's Ford pickup into Doug's truck box at over 100 kilometers an hour. We thought that was a real blast. I never considered just how dangerous the stunt really was. What if I'd fallen on the 401?

Getting back into town from our marathon trip, we fell asleep at the same time, only to wake up when we crashed into the curb, narrowly missing the hydro pole . . .

But now I watch my buddy leave, walk into the light of day . . . his footsteps echo in the dim corridor . . . such a grim reminder of my dreadful reality . . . my loneliness . . . isolation . . . I'm all alone . . . afraid . . . caught and helpless . . .

The screw reappears and slides a pencil and two sheets of paper under my door. So the stupid warden thinks he's going to be getting a letter? He's nuts if he thinks I'm going to ask him any favors. Never. It'll never happen. I'll just sit here in my cell and work on my word power. I can sit in this cold and empty cage for many more years . . . I'm a veteran of the war. I'll wait . . .

Freedom revoked, 1976

As I walk up the wide concrete steps and into the courtroom built like a cathedral, I'm nervous. The butterflies before a boxing bout pale in comparison to the knots of anxiety twisting my gut in the courtroom. Lawyers are strolling along in their three-piece suits, conversing in language beyond my comprehension, and this only serves to deepen my festering apprehension. God knows what they're saying.

My lawyer, a short, black-bearded Jewish fellow, is trying to reassure me that a guilty plea is the best way to get a light sentence for my charge of auto theft. I'm wondering how I can plead any other way, since it's obvious I'm guilty.

A hush falls on the spacious courtroom as the bespectacled clerk announces in a sullen voice that the judge is about to enter. As I stand with as much confidence as the dying can summon, my knees tremble.

The cases before mine seem endless. I'm shocked at the amount of crime in our small community. The young and the old, women and men and even young teens are being pushed through as I watch in astonishment and wonder. Names are read, and the accused stroll to the front of the court as the lawyers speak on their behalf. The judge says only a few words, which surprises me a great deal. There sits a man in a black robe who I know as the father of one of my schoolmates.

The day wears on and I wonder when my fate will be decided. Not a soul has been sent to jail, so I feel mildly reassured I'll escape prison. The hour strikes 4 as I stare blankly at my lawyer, the Crown and the judge. Then the three of them begin addressing my case.

The judge looks directly at me and asks me to rise. His eyes are as clear as water and seem

extremely stern. Through thin lips, he asks what my
plea will be and my lawyer promptly reminds and
advises me to plead guilty. I'm pleading guilty to
auto theft. Did I understand the verdict, the judge
asks, and I say that I do.

The learned judge gives me thirty days in jail.
Then he rises and leaves the courtroom.

I'm bewildered. I can't believe he's sending me to
prison.

The police officers seem to come out of hiding as
they lay hold of my arms and begin to lead me out of
the courtroom. I am handcuffed behind my back.

The police escort me through an underground
tunnel that connects the courthouse to the jail.
There is no more hope. I am no longer free . . .

I could write like those damn lawyers if I want, but
I'm certainly not writing a letter to that whimpering
warden unless it's a letter denouncing the unconstitutional practices so common in this insane asylum.
Maybe I should write him and his heads of security a
threatening letter. I can compose a whole lot of
double entendres and issue veiled threats in this
way. That would confuse them and give them food
for thought.

13

Prison Prey

The screw returns and orders me to face the back of my cell. They won't open my food slot unless I'm out of striking distance. They don't want to have dirty water, cups of piss or bags of shit thrown at them. The way I see it, they feed me shit in the bag and they get the same diet in return. I'm laughing. I know I can smash them when I shower, cuffs or no cuffs.

The idiot is standing in a pool of piss. I've been urinating through the crack of my door because I must keep the toilet water clean. That water has come in handy a few times since my sink was disabled. I've been able to wash the mace off my chest and even drink the stuff.

My hands flat on the cold cinder blocks, I hear the brown paper bag pass through my food slot and splat on the floor. Passing my hands across the smooth surface of my wall, I reflect that I've counted these bricks before. My home is seven feet wide, nine feet long and twelve feet high. Give or take a brick.

The paint is starting to peel, and I think I'll take off another layer of this dull yellow color. I bet I can peel the whole surface before I'm released. That's what I'll do. It's better than marking the walls and crossing out days like in the movies. I don't know why anyone would want to count days. That's crazy.

My food slot slams shut. I hear the key turning the tumblers. Good, the dummy is gone. I don't want to see his ugly face.

This damn place. Four hundred days . . . but some holes are tougher than this. I've seen many variations of the hole . . .

First bit, 1976

Shuddering and shocked, I walk silently through the narrow underground tunnel that connects the courthouse to the prison. I can't stop thinking about what just happened. I'm baffled. What's going to happen to me now? What's this underground network linking me to? This is surely hell. It's cold and our footsteps bounce off hard concrete walls. Every step is taking me farther away from the world outside.

This is foreign territory.

The dimly lit tunnel swallows me whole. With a

police officer at either side, I can't do a thing. I want
to run back and talk to the judge, but it's too late for
that now. He left so abruptly after sealing my fate to
this dungeon. Thirty days in this dark cavern is
harsh. How will he sleep, knowing he sent me here?
I was just a drunk kid, and it wasn't even my idea to
steal the stupid car.

We come to a stop at the door of the jail. I can
hear faint sounds of footsteps coming from inside. I
peer through the bars and see an old screw turn the
corner in the dimly lit corridor. He seemed to come
right out of the walls!

He's thick and overweight and his gray garments
stick oddly to his potbellied frame. As he walks, his
huge black army boots echo hollowly in the empty
cave.

As the officers remove my cuffs, the old screw
asks me to put my hands through the bars as he
produces a set of his own cuffs. Once the cool metal
is wrapped around my wrists, he swings the door of
the dungeon wide open.

Walking alongside the guard, I follow him
through a labyrinth of corridors. As I am taken
deeper into the putrid bowels of this prison, I feel
my chest tighten in anxiety at every turn and my
heart leap with every clang of a steel door.

The place is not fit for animals. There's neither

sunshine nor fresh air. Dull gray walls wrap themselves around my body, and the sickly off-green-colored bars shoot right through me. The floors are patterned in the same way as hospitals and the smell of antiseptic fills my nostrils.

We arrive at a large holding pen and the old screw sits down at a desk across from it. Letting out a heavy sigh, he slides a long sheet of paper into his old Olivetti. The routine questions are pouring out of his mouth as I struggle to focus. He asks me about my next of kin, date of birth, financial background, crime, education, religion, eye and hair color, tattoos or any distinguishing characteristic.

I begin to wonder what class my family belongs to. Am I middle-class, lower-class or what? And who is my next of kin? Fear grips my chest. Why is a next of kin required? Am I going to die in here?

Struggling to his feet, the old screw grunts that I should follow him into a cramped office where old filing cabinets line the walls and a thin wire cage is filled with damp and weather-beaten brown boxes.

While I sit on a tiny steel tripod, I grasp a plastic number board and place it across my chest and my mug shot is snapped with a Polaroid. I get the feeling I'm now one of the most-wanted criminals seen so often on television. I realize why none of these guys ever smile in such photo opportunities.

Jumping off the seat, I glance at the Shannon Tweed centerfold pasted on the dull yellow wall. Did I smile for the side shoot? Somehow I don't think so.

Fingerprinting follows as the screw expertly rolls my fingers one at a time through inkpads and onto paper. Wiping the dark ink from my fingertips with paper towels, I reflect that fingerprinting must be done for security reasons. Dread and worry wash over me. Could I become a victim of a heinous and bloody crime while I'm doing my time? Could I be killed, disfigured, maimed or crippled in here?

Finished with the drill, I'm stripped of all my personal effects and watch the screw place my meager belongings in a small canvas bag similar to those used for night bank deposits.

Then I'm tossed into the shower. I'm certain a lot of guys have been violated in this wide-open cubicle. There's no privacy at all. It's a natural haven for assault as far as I'm concerned. I'm a shy kid and I'm worried. I emerge quickly from my shower and I'm led into a large cell holding a dozen cons.

The old cons display twisting, colorful tattoos on large biceps and chain-smoke hand-rolled cigarettes that dangle from tobacco-stained fingers. Their pallid, expressionless faces bear witness to months and perhaps years of hard lockup.

Many of the younger cons huddle together, while two old winos slump on the black-spotted concrete floor. Their voices are low as they cast furtive looks in my direction.

A few cons are seated on the cold concrete floor against the wall in cross-legged positions or arms hugging their knees to their chest. Others rest on their backs in the corner, while still another lies sleeping on a pale green wooden bench.

The scene looks like something out of a horror movie . . . there's something more about these figures—they seem so . . . lost and crazed.

The air is thick with the odor of stale cigarette smoke. Empty stares dart in my direction. I dare not hold anyone's gaze.

What the hell are they thinking? Why don't they say something? What am I supposed to do now? The place is so damn small—where can I sit? Nobody gives a shit. Thoughtless and selfish bastards. I'll have to pick a place on the floor, since the benches are full.

The old duty guard returns and begins to bark names. I hear my last name and I'm led to a station to pick up a blanket roll, T-shirt, towel, toothbrush and toothpaste. Hugging the gray flannel blanket close to my chest, I proceed up two flights of green concrete stairs.

As I enter a corridor, I cast my eye down its

narrow length. I can't believe what I'm seeing.
These hallways are not suited for living. The living
quarters are cramped, narrow enclosures reminis-
cent of very short school hallways—no bigger.
Unbelievable. It's unthinkable to have so many men
occupying quarters so small.

The cellblocks of the Sudbury jail are filled to
capacity. I'm amazed at the number of people in jail.
How can people live in such confining quarters?
Surely the cons don't spend twenty-four hours a day
in here?

Deeper . . . deeper . . . deeper—the noise and echo
get louder as we go. As I take in the artificial light,
darkened windows and gray floors, nervousness
cramps my stomach. Shit. I know I'll be hurt in this
hellhole—I just know it. I can feel it in my bones.

Arriving at one of the countless cellblocks amid
the labyrinth of corridors, the fat old screw swings
open the steel-barred door leading to a small and
cramped living area. I'm not going there, am I? The
place is packed and these guys look crazy. I'm a
120-pound, sixteen-year-old kid, and they'll be
putting me in here with these guys? Fear grips my
chest. This is where they live—where I live. No
room, no damn space—this can't be.

Standing beside the big old screw in the narrow
catwalk, I look through the steel bars down the

length of the packed cellblock. Huge, ugly cons strut
around the cramped area like wild and crazy
animals. Six footers with thick arms and barrel
chests at every turn, their tattoos and hard glares
are everywhere. I can't go in there alone. The whole
block can't be more than forty feet long and twelve
feet wide. The cells are set inside it like starting
stalls in a horse race. They're locked, but nobody's
inside—the guys are roaming around the range,
strutting . . . staring.

I step inside and the steel-barred door slams shut.
A horrible feeling shoots through me. Standing
motionless in temporary shock, I begin shuffling
nervously past the cells. I must occupy one of these,
but which one? The screw said number 3? Where
the hell is that hole in the wall?

Trying to ignore the eyes, I begin reading the cell
numbers inked on the top of the narrow steel bar
running horizontally across the cells. Number 12,
11, 10, 9, 8 . . . deeper and deeper into this godforsaken range, past the eyes . . .

Oh, no. Despair steals over me. I'm to share this
cell. Two bunks. My fear deepens with every
passing moment.

Dropping my issue through the bars and onto the
top bunk, I turn slowly around, look down the
narrow length of the small range and am assaulted

by several sets of eyes. Their cells locked, some of
the guys are seated on two shiny metal picnic tables.
They're staring at me like I'm some alien from outer
space.

Following my every movement, the cons turn
slightly sideways while others stand with their arms
hanging at their sides like apes. The cons stare at
me like vultures. They don't say a word or even nod
a head. No smile, no friendly gesture, nothing. They
just gawk. Why couldn't someone smile or say
something?

Nervousness stirs again in the pit of my stomach.
I feel their eyes burn into the back of my head.
Anxiety and a deathly silence are closing in on me
already.

What am I going to do? Where do I go and what
can I say? I'm done, man. Cooked big-time.
Nowhere to run.

I can't shake the feeling that many sets of eyes
are burning into my back. I feel like the lamb being
led to the slaughter. I have no idea when the knives
will come out. I can't shake the feeling that violence
is coming. I wonder what I'll do when the cons come
for me. I can sense it. These madmen do not look
like a welcoming committee. My gut perceives
danger. This sucks . . . can't crumble . . . keep alert
. . . must remain aware.

Exiting the cramped washroom at the end of the

small range, I come face to face with three cons. I'm going to be hurt and I know it. Why? What the hell is it with these guys? A tall redhead has a sneer on his face and an ugly, arrogant look. Flanked by two others, he struts with an exaggerated air.

Petrified, I back up. Their eyes are burning into mine. What have I done, for God's sake? The redhead is saying something, but I can't hear what. I'm focused on his movements. Can't crumble, Ritchy . . .

The redhead assumes a boxing stance. This triggers my trained boxing instincts. His friends fade into the distance. He's not moving, but his friends are urging him on in the background. My hands tremble and my stomach churns with anxiety.

He throws a hard right sucker punch at my face. He wants to knock my teeth out.

I duck and his knuckles crash into the steel bars inches above my head. Wincing, he pulls his hand toward his body and clasps it with his left.

Anger replaces fear.

Remaining in my crouch, I shoot my right hand out into his stomach. The redhead exhales loudly and doubles over. Mind reeling, body still in motion, I deliver a left hook to the side of his pockmarked face. That blow rocks his head to the side as his eyes squeeze in pain.

Black. I'm seeing black, and the fury erupts.

That's it. I'm no longer afraid of what his friends might do. I will do whatever it takes—kick, punch, bite and poke eyes out, anything to get away from these goons.

I'm pumped and I'm ready. My body's tense; my energy surges. I'll hit and fight until I go out.

The goons hesitate. They look shocked and are silenced. Anger is running through me and I want to finish this off once and for all. I'm pissed.

Screaming at the top of my lungs, I run to the picnic table in the middle of the range and pick up a few plastic cups and fling them at my antagonists. They stare at me. I'm yelling louder now and I'm out of control. The fear is gone.

The goon squad arrives on the scene. I hadn't noticed the screw peering into the cellblock nor heard him trying to calm me. Many arms seize me and drag me out of the cellblock. The screws are breathing heavily. They have to rest before dragging me another few yards.

I'm slammed in the hole for seven long days, eating nothing but dry bean cake. An overhead camera is in my face twenty-four hours a day. I pace my barren solitary cell with nothing on but a garment like a hospital robe . . .

Maybe I should write the warden and tell him his punitive measures are more fitting for juveniles than real hard men like me. This is nothing. I've been through the ropes. Ripping open my brown paper bag, I pull my bologna sandwich out of its waxed covering. This is better than dry bean cake. I can live on this stuff for years. The screws won't get food like this in my prison, and that's a certainty.

14

Codes of Conduct

One, two, three, four, five and a half steps and turn; one, two, three, four, five and a half steps and turn; one, two, three, four, five and a half steps and, turning, my right shoulder brushes gently against the brick wall. Opening my eyes, I spin by my door.

I can pace this cell with my eyes closed for hours and I hardly ever bump into a wall. Must have taken a long fifth step or something. The heels of my feet are calloused and hard. I doubt I'd be hurt if I were to step on a pointed object. The needle would probably bend against the hard brown skin.

How many miles can I travel in the time I spend pacing the hole? Ten, twenty miles a day? I bet I can if I walk for eight hours. Yes, it took me how many hours to complete the walkathon for the United Way back home? Eight hours?

Oh, well, I suppose when I get tired of walking I can talk to some of the guys, but what am I going to say? How are you? I don't think so. Forget it, I won't say anything to anybody.

Maybe I can work out again . . . nah, I get too damn sweaty and start to stink . . . then again, I've taken more than one sponge bath in my toilet over the years. I don't like talking to myself like this, but what can I do about it? No big deal, I think the trouble starts if I hear voices or I respond to myself. Well, I don't hear any voices and I'm aware of what's happening.

Do I know what's happening? What's the stupid parole board going to do with my case? Are they going to gate me? I fit their stupid criteria. In fact, the first two criteria are . . . screeching to a halt, I pick the papers from the parole board up from my cot. Let me read that damn thing again. Oh, yes . . . murder and armed robbery conviction. I've got both.

The stupid thing goes on to say I'm likely to commit a serious offense causing death or serious bodily injury to persons once I'm released. Of that you could be certain. But how can you prove intent and the possibility of reoffending? Is my past an accurate yardstick to determine my propensity for recidivism? It's my stupid classification officer that's referred my case, and I've hardly ever seen or spoken to that bitch. She's not qualified to assess my case.

So what if I possess a horrid institutional record?

How many convictions in your kangaroo court over the last seven years? A hundred? More? I've spent over 400 days in your holes.

I'm pacing rapidly, and my heart is beating quickly. My arms are becoming tense and my mind is reeling. I'm getting dizzy. The joint's damn security matrix has ranked me as high-risk and classed me as a violent con. I've been suspected of several takedowns around here. Suspicious of being suspicious? Waterheads.

What's that little psycho in the next cell thinking? I'm in a bad situation now. The parole board will surely gate me if I get violent with him, but he's giving me no choice in the matter. Slamming that little bastard would convince the board of my violence. Yet I can't let him come at me with a pointed blade and do nothing to defend myself. I heard him sharpening something and I'm sure of it. I'm not coming out of this shithouse in a pine box like so many others.

Eighteen more months if they're successful in their application to gate me. I'll flatten it out in the hole for sure. I've heard of guys serving two years in the hole. Big Mike and Franky spent two years in the hole for being suspects in a murder in here. If they can do it, so can I.

Some of the guys are more violent than I am and have much more horrific records. I've seen them operate. They approach and provoke me and then discover they haven't the will and ability to finish me off. Steve got a swift kick in the face when he dared to jump in front of me in the supper line. My right foot left the ground and smashed into his cheek with such force that he was stunned for a few moments. The idiot has to be aware of what the hell he's doing at all times. Someone else might have driven a shank into his ribs. I may have saved his life with that lesson.

Ralph had his nose broken, but it could have been worse if I had been someone else. An elbow smash to the face and he fell heavily to the ground, but he was all right soon thereafter. He knew he screwed up.

Jimmy lost a couple of teeth with a good solid right hand, but at least I never killed him. Mike had his jaw shattered, but that's nothing in here. Jerry, meanwhile, had his ribs fractured and his eyes blackened. So what? It was something that had to be done. These are the damn codes.

If I allow myself to be stomped on, I'll be killed myself. What do they expect me to do when I'm faced with such a fervor to kill? I'm being observed all the time. The guys know I'm quiet, but they like to test my ability and conviction. I think they get bored and frustrated and create chaos to disturb the mind-numbing atmosphere around here. And they risk their lives doing so.

The kid with the sharpened toothbrush next door is a classic example. He messed up. Now he's going to get hurt because of his inability to swallow false pride. I have the might of right on my side and I'll emerge victorious. I know what I'll do. I'm lightning fast and hit like a damn truck. He's done big-time. I'm not afraid of him, I'm afraid of my anger and what I'll do to him if he dares come to the yard with me.

I won't say anything to him through closed doors, but he's sealed his fate with his rash and reckless words. He's put me in a position where I must act, and act swiftly. The other guys heard his threats. I'm committed. He's crossed me.

It's going to be messy and brutal when I see him. I'll say nothing. I'll approach him and we will get down and dirty.

The parole board is going to gate me for certain after this one, so I may as well make it worthwhile. I can't risk giving him the opportunity to retaliate later.

Maybe my damaging rap sheet and joint record can bury me. But they don't understand the codes we have to live by to ensure our survival. By virtue of having to adhere, we label ourselves dangerous offenders. What else would you idiots have me do? Get killed? Rat out? Go to protective custody? I'll never check in and spend my time with rats, pedophiles and rapists. I would smash them all and have to stay in the hole forever . . . it's a lose-lose situation here . . .

The subculture, 1976 to 1980

My rap sheet pales in comparison to what my new-found peers have been up to. The rounders have been in places I've only heard about through my brother: the provincial reformatories with their respective security levels and some federal penitentiaries located in Kingston.

I wonder how these guys could end up serving so much time locked up in these facilities. I'm convinced I'm much smarter than they and I'll never allow myself to suffer such a dreadful fate.

I've also become aware of the reputation that is granted according to the amount of time a con spends and where he spends it. There's also a belief that people proceed through the prison system through an established route, beginning at the minimum-security provincial level and moving into the maximum-security federal pen system.

Everyone I meet is progressing through the system at various rates. The smartest criminal postpones the inevitable the longest. The very smartest avoid the pen altogether. Some guys visit the pen at the age of twenty while others see inside the walls at thirty.

I learn about Monteith, Maplehurst, Guelph and Millbrook provincial reformatories. These are prisons you could expect to visit as early as sixteen, and surely before you hit twenty. I'm mentally prepared to go to Millbrook, a maximum-security provincial institution, and call it quits. I know in my heart I'll end up there, I just don't know when it will happen. I figure I could beat my peers and not see Millbrook until I'm in my mid to late twenties.

The guys comment on how lucky I am to be avoiding the reformatory. I'm only serving short sentences in the local jail. I never receive a sentence in excess of three months, which is the cutoff for transfer to a provincial facility.

I believe I'll never be caught. Not for anything serious anyway, and if I am, so what? I'll do my eighteen months in Millbrook and hang up my balaclava and quit my partying then.

I've accepted that I could receive a few short provincial sentences before being hit with eighteen months. Inside, I know I'm ready to proceed up to Millbrook. It's a kind of insane goal.

I get submerged in the subculture and begin to understand and adopt the criminal and street mentality very well.

I learn the codes and live by them religiously. Cops are the enemy. Being solid is a priority, and not to be compromised. Lawyers are my servants and should never be told the truth about anything, since they will fight harder for the innocent.

Junkies should never be trusted. These guys will rat out their mother for a fix. Never involve others if you get caught, because only one person accepts the responsibility of doing time. Why should two guys go down for the same beef? When picked up for questioning, ask to call a lawyer and don't say another word. Don't sign anything is the cardinal rule.

Selling drugs is my main source of revenue on the street. When I run out of my own dope supply, I play the middleman between the many buyers and the host of dealers. When the dope market runs dry, I fence stolen merchandise. I keep a few shoplifters very busy in the many department stores in town. Grocery stores are also being ripped off as carts of expensive meats are rolled out the front doors.

Break and enters keep me occupied too. Sneaking through windows late at night, I call my friendly driver and drive away with televisions and stereo equipment that fill the truck.

Drug dealers and buyers are targets for ripoffs when my brokering is sparse. Stealing dope from the dealers and ripping off the buyers for their dirty cash is a very risky proposition. I almost get seriously beat up and even killed on a couple of these deals.

My criminal convictions mount as I near my

twentieth birthday. Many of these stem from drunken fights at local taverns and parties. I have a tendency to cause disturbances and break anything in sight when I'm drunk. I'm a ticking time bomb looking for places to explode. I fight almost every weekend at various taverns.

At twenty, I haven't even smelled the bowels of a reformatory. By this time, every member of our gang has seen the reformatories and some have even been sent to the pen. When they're released, the pen-timers tell me stories about their time that convey that it isn't so bad.

They say a guy could do his own time inside as long as he minds his own business. They talk about the solidarity among the cons and the codes behind the walls. It all sounds very strange. As far as I'm concerned, my departure point and limit is still the magic number of eighteen months in Millbrook.

As 1980 rolls into 1981, I still smell like roses. By this time, I'm partying all over the place and am well known to the authorities. I have a reputation as a street fighter. The crew likes to instigate a few fights to beat the boredom. Some of these fights are pretty messy and get wild at times. In fact, some of them are severe enough to warrant headlines. At one party, at least six people were hospitalized.

I'm barred from every hotel in town at least four times over. Nobody feels safe in my presence. I'm totally unpredictable. I could joke with a person one minute and in the next instant smash my fist into his face. The guys joke with me and call me a grizzly bear because of my unpredictable behavior. I joke back that I'm predictably unpredictable.

Girls are commodities, and sleeping with as many as possible is an ongoing competition. I get a few sexually transmitted diseases in the process. I discover that some of the prettiest are the dirtiest.

Boat motors, snow blowers, power tools and everything else is lifted and sold. My fence is a big fat man, 400 pounds, who's as tight as a new clip of twenties.

The fights scare me at times. I put men in comas in a fistfight on two different occasions and almost blind someone else. I like to mix it up and fight with bottles of wine and liquor. I break full bottles on heads, smash glasses into people's faces and sucker punch anyone who looks at me the wrong way . . .

Maybe the authorities have a solid case for the gating application after all. But they don't understand. The screws are setting me up and making me look crazier than I am. What do they have on file that I haven't seen? What kind of bullshit have they written there? I can only imagine, with two special-handling unit applications against me.

Sure, there were a few broken noses and cracked jaws, a few escape attempts, I witnessed some takedowns and knew of major drug deals inside, but that's no big deal in here, man. What's all the fuss about? I never killed anyone in here, or even hurt them that bad. It was either take them out or be murdered. I know how to survive here.

I bet the idiots are pissed off because of the riots, sit-downs, hunger strikes, work stoppages and incitements I've caused.

Wait. How do they know I'm going to kill them? They always get threatened, so that's nothing new. Somehow, I'm more convincing. They know what they've done, don't they? Self-preservation is spurred by fear. They're scared . . .

My brother Mike, 1977

Fear is the name of the game, says my older brother Mike as he pulls three large dynamite sticks from behind the pile of wet rags and boxes in the basement. The reddish sticks are about eighteen inches long and three inches around. The sight of them sends a chill down my spine. Placing them carefully in his black leather jacket, he makes his way toward the front door.

What in God's name is he going to do with those?

Only two weeks before, Mike had beat up my buddy Dan so bad with a baseball bat that I didn't recognize him. Dan's face was black and blue and swollen out of proportion.

Mike's always been violent and crazy, but ever since he got out of Millbrook Correctional Centre, he's been a lot worse. Even I'm scared to piss him off. Just last week, he made a grab for the axe when we were arguing about something stupid. It's a good thing I managed to grab him and wrestle him to the ground and calm him before he got hold of it. He probably would have hit me with it. His eyes were black and . . . and distanced.

The fights at the parties are brutal. Mike likes to hit people with beer bottles, chairs, sticks, anything. I swear he's going to kill someone. We're in competition to see who can knock out more guys. I do it with my hands and feet, but he does it with weapons . . .

15

Taken Down

My mind is wandering; I better try and focus on what's going on around here. I must stay in the here and now lest they keep me for the rest of my life. They've set their snare. Throughout many long years, they've provoked and antagonized me, and now they want to label me a dangerous offender to keep me locked up. Our history is long and varied, but one element has remained static over these many years. Them and us. They have the corrupt power to pull the strings; we have the might and will to survive.

From top to bottom, the whole system is geared to tyrannize and oppress. After three days in this shithouse, I'd incurred twelve institutional offenses. They set me up and carried out personal vendettas. But I'll get out, and then I'll show them what oppression and tyranny is all about. I don't fear death, but these rotten screws cherish their existence.

What I've seen and tasted, most men never witness; even my fellow cons remain blind in some

respects. My perceptions are clear and my inten-
tions natural. My jailors have no right to treat me so
callously. Where's objectivity, and where are the
impartial watchdog committees to put a stop to this
reign of terror?

I drink water from toilet bowls. I am subject to a
brutal and desensitizing regime. They're creating a
monster. I sport chains as women wear jewelry. I
fight in the trenches like a man of war, but with no
clear picture of who's lurking behind enemy lines.
The hypocrisy of this place is obvious. The draconian
measures and human violations are well guarded.

It's been 2,500 days of complete insanity, with
countless life-threatening confrontations and 400
days in the hole. Hatred, anger and fury have been
my only companions. If people only knew what
happens in here, they would reconsider the value of
corrections and rehabilitation.

I'm human and I will spiral into this dark abyss of
madness. Who wouldn't? People will understand
why I'll kill these pricks when I get out.

The screw approaches my cell for his regular
count. I'll hide behind the wall and disrupt it. The
jerk knows I'm here, but he has to see me. Where
could I go, idiot box? Are they ever stupid. I'm not
showing myself. I stay still. You'll have to open my
door and wrestle again. Bring on the goon squad, the
gas and the billy clubs.

The screw curses under his breath and walks away. I hear him on the phone. The goon squad will be coming soon. What will I do to scare them this time?

I'll pretend I'm dead. I'll wrap my shirt around my neck and pretend I suffocated myself. When they approach, I'll grab the bastards by their shirtfronts, spit in their faces and lash out with my sharpened pencil. I'll threaten them with death and promise to move to Kingston when I'm released in just a few days. That should sober them up a bit, give them something to think about. I'm really going to kill the whole stinking lot of them . . .

Bar brawl, 1981

I wake up at noon and start drinking everything I can get my hands on. At 6 or 7 that night, I walk into a crowded rock 'n' roll bar that's part of a hotel. I'm pounding back the drinks and having a merry old time. I'm sitting with three lovely ladies and I want to take them all home with me.

As the evening wears on, an older gentleman joins us. This sucker is quite generous about buying drinks for the table. I figure he enjoys my lady friends, because this guy isn't cheap. Sit down and buy a round, chump.

Later in the evening, the man says he has some

liquor upstairs in his room and wonders if my lady friends and I would join him for more drinks? I'm certainly into it, so I accept.

Without another thought, I accompany the man up to his room to drink with him. I guess my lady friends are doing fine, because they don't come along.

When we get to the room, I find out he doesn't have any liquor. I begin to fear him. He's only of average height, but he must weigh in at 250. I'm drunk, but I feel my body tense. I don't know what's coming, but I must protect myself. My mind goes into a kind of dark fury.

Suddenly, he's in my face. I hit him, a hard right to the side of his head. He sways a bit and starts to collapse at the knees. Then his huge bulk hits the floor with a dull thud. I stare at him in disbelief. Blood and spittle bubble from his mouth. His eyes show surprise and defeat . . .

When I finally get home, I show my brother the blood on my shirt and tell him about the fight, and he advises me to call an ambulance. He says the guy might be seriously hurt. I ignore him . . .

The next day, my girlfriend and I are walking downtown on a beautiful sunny day when a car screeches to a halt a few feet away. Three detectives jump out of the unmarked vehicle and circle me.

My girlfriend backs away in fear. Keeping my

eyes on the anxious-looking detectives, I stand
motionless. They move in on me.

A tall detective with high cheekbones orders me
into the car. I look squarely into his anxious gray
eyes and ask if I'm under arrest. He doesn't answer.

A big blond rookie with biceps spilling out of his
white short-sleeved shirt reaches out to grab me.
His huge paw covers my whole upper arm. An
older-looking policeman with short gray hair and a
thin moustache comes up behind and starts pushing
at my back as the clean-cut cop holds my head
down.

The dark-blue sedan quickly speeds away,
leaving my girlfriend in shock and bewilderment.
The detectives begin to question me.

Pulling into the police station, the officers step up
the intensity of their interrogation. I'm searched
and tossed into the dark and damp holding cells,
where the stench of urine and vomit fills the air.
Nothing new about this, except this time a skinny,
gray-haired detective with a receding hairline is
sitting cross-legged on a blue plastic chair in front
of my cell. He just stares and stays silent.

Ignoring him, I lie quietly on my checkered steel
cot and begin to reflect on how earnest the cops
have been during my arrest. And what about this
detective in front of my cell? What the hell is he
doing here with the notepad on his knees?

Then three uniformed police converge on my cell and drag me to an interrogation room upstairs. It's not a custom of mine to leave my cell willingly, so I have to be dragged. When they get me into the "hot room," I catch sight of a table in a corner with papers and pens at hand.

I figure they're going to try to get me to talk. They've never tried to get me to talk before, so why are they trying now? They know I'd never say anything.

The detectives sit me down on a small wooden chair and begin their interrogation. It doesn't take very long for them to start getting frustrated. At every question they ask, I tell them I want to call a lawyer. They take turns trying to intimidate, coerce and cajole me. Surrounded by brick and mortar, I watch them persist in their head games.

Tiring of my silence, they drag me back to my dingy cell. The Gestapo won't allow me my phone call and I'll say nothing except to request to call a lawyer. And when I do get a lawyer, I'll ask him to get me out. Or I'll wait in jail and find out what evidence the Crown and police have against me before I say anything to anybody.

The whole scenario replays all night long and continues into the small hours of the morning. I'm being bounced to and fro, into different rooms and back to my cell.

In one of these trips around the police station, I'm
led into a lineup. Fed up, and disgusted at not
having an opportunity to call my lawyer, I decide to
lie down on the floor during the process of identification. This infuriates the cops, but I figure they're
burying themselves deeper every time they breach
my rights.

On another grand tour of the famous cop shop,
the policemen produce a three- by five-inch photo
of the man I beat up the night before. I slap it out of
the detective's hand. Outraged, he grabs a handful
of my hair and screams at me, inches from my face.
I look directly at him and tell him I'll defend myself
if they decide to get rough.

But I'm worried after seeing the picture. Maybe
I'm going to be charged for assault.

The games persist and no one tells me why I'm in
custody. The night just wears on and on . . .

The wall is cold against my back. Yes, I've been
cornered before. So what . . . . My shirt is firmly in
place, eyes rolled back, I look dead for certain. I'm
going to scare the living shit out of these rats. The
pencil is going to terrorize the goons . . .

*Placing the pencil between my forefinger and index
finger, I close my hand and make a fist. The damn
point can penetrate his eye and pierce his brain.*

Thrusting my hand out quickly, gray matter spills out. Yelling in agony, the big goon stiffens in terror and pain . . . my foot slams into his balls and he doubles over . . .

There's panic and chaos. I'll have to take out as many of them as I can before they subdue or kill me.

Running over to the steel barrier, I block the door of the hole . . . the screws are my prisoners now . . . three more buttheads to go . . . I wonder if I can hit hard and fast enough to get them all . . .

The sucker lunges desperately for the panic button as I slam my elbow into his square jaw . . . his big head snaps back . . . I grab a handful of his thick mane and place the palm of my hand on his chin . . . twisting as hard and as fast as I can, I hear his scrawny neck snap like a twig . . . not a sound more . . . he falls heavily to the floor . . .

Shit . . . my food slot opens with a loud clang and the screws tell me they're going to tear-gas me. They're not going to risk coming in this time.

My 16th birthday.
I was a pitcher on our baseball team.

I have just arrived at Millhaven. I smashed the office at Collins Bay just a couple of weeks before.

Posing at the Haven. I could use the glare from my head to blind my opponents.

My cousin Louis, who taught me the ropes inside Millhaven. He was brutally murdered by two cowards.

16

Arraigned

My plan isn't working . . . damn it. I've smelled and tasted tear gas before and it's brutal. I better get up and show my face. Leaving the shirt wrapped loosely around my neck, I slide off my bunk. Looking through the four- by eight-inch food slot, I don't see a tear gas gun.

Suddenly, a red nozzle that squeezes out 300 pounds of pressure per square inch is thrust through the slot and spews a powerful jet of ice-cold water. The stream slams into my chest with such force that I'm thrown three feet to the back of my cell. The water stings my bare chest. I close my eyes and turn my body in different positions. Holy shit, this is fun. I'm getting a damned shower after all . . . but it's starting to hurt big-time. I reach for my thin mattress and use it as a shield.

The water soaks my whole cell. I'm splashing around in water up to my ankles, my clothes are soaked and the water-laden mattress is dead weight.

My arms burn and my shoulders ache from trying to keep the mattress in a defensive position. I can barely hold the weight anymore, so I make a move for the corner of my bed. The spray can't reach here. Let them come and get me, the retards . . . where's that pencil?

My cell door slides open and the shuffling of many feet invades my home. The famous mace gun appears and the screws threaten to shoot me again. Standing on my bunk, I decide to step down and let them wrestle me some more.

As I step to the floor, hands grope everywhere . . . I'm being stripped of everything. My pants are cut off with oversized scissors and my shirt is tossed into the corridor.

As my mattress is dragged out, guys in adjacent cells begin to react. Good . . . I hear the toilets overflowing and the doors banging. Party time, guys. Give these assholes something to work for. Flood your cells, refuse to go back to your cells after showering or being out in the yard, spit at them, throw your hot coffee in the screws' filthy faces, piss out of the cracks of your doors, throw shit at them, threaten them, revolt, *vive la révolution, les gars*.

Even the neighbor I'll have to hurt is in line with me now. We have our hatred and fury in common. Yell at the tyrants some more. Let us raise our voices and sound our murderous rage throughout this putrid hellhole. Will somebody please kill one of these screws? Some of you are doing forever in here and you have nothing to lose. Let us not kill one another, but these real enemies.

The screws rush out of my cell and the door slams shut. I walk to the back of my cell and then charge my door. I slam into the hollow metal surface and the reverberating crash explodes in my mind. The guys in population must have heard that one. I'll tear your arms off and beat your heads in. I'll rip your throats out with my bare hands and stuff your mouths with your guts. I'm black with fury . . .

The shocker, 1981

I'm cuffed, placed in the back of a cruiser and driven to the courthouse a few blocks up the street. My appearance is haggard and my body fatigued. Escorted to the prisoner's box in a mental fog, I settle into the glass enclosure behind the oak parti-tion. Squinting through bloodshot eyes, I scan the courtroom and see my brother, sister and girlfriend looking on. I try smiling, but it won't come.

I still haven't been informed of the charges at this point, so when the court-appointed lawyer approaches me in the prisoner's box, I can't tell him what I'm being held for. This short, stout fellow with a receding hairline raises an eyebrow and indi-

cates he'll speak to the Crown attorney and return
with an answer. I watch him intently as he strides
toward the Crown attorney's paper-filled desk. The
two exchange a few words and my little advocate
returns to my box with great news. He says the
court has no charges pending. I picture myself
walking home in the next few moments. I've outwit-
ted and outlasted my captors. Eat humble pie and
egg in your face. I cast a glance at my brother and
smile victoriously. He winks with understanding
and satisfaction.

The sound of shuffling announces the entry of the
judge. We all stand as the clerk solemnly declares
that court is in session.

I sit back down in the prisoner's box and watch
the learned judge rummage through the papers on
his desk. Then he looks down his large bench at the
Crown attorney and asks why I'm in custody. The
judge goes on to say that he has no charges before
him and that he is perplexed over the entire affair.

Equally baffled, the Crown attorney responds by
saying he too has no indication as to why I'm in the
prisoner's box. My lawyer reiterates their remarks—
and I'm not about to tell them I beat a guy up two
nights ago.

I sense the judge is about to end the session and
pronounce me free to go when his attention is distracted by a noise at the back of the courtroom. Two

uniformed policemen have entered and are gesticulating in the direction of the Crown attorney. The Crown begs the judge's indulgence as the police hand him some papers.

Reading the papers brought to him, the Crown leisurely gets up and strolls toward the judge.

As the Crown hands the judge the papers, I try to read his features, but I can't discern them. My lawyer is looking around the court and shuffling uncomfortably in his seat. I get quite apprehensive as the judge reads the papers. I'm trying desperately to get a message somewhere.

Placing the papers in a neat pile before him, the judge looks at me sternly and begins to speak. Peering over his reading glasses, he asks me to remain seated for the reading of the charge. That's extremely unusual; I've always been asked to stand for the reading of the charges. The judge's deep blue eyes stare deeply into my own. He's looking straight through me.

"On or about the eleventh day of May, in the district of Sudbury, in the said regional municipality, the said accused, Richard Dubé, is charged with first-degree murder . . . "

What . . . what . . . first-degree murder? Wait a minute . . . God . . . NOOOO . . . this can't be . . . despair . . . heart-wrenching . . . black . . . my world is black . . . the silence . . . a football in my stomach

. . . the utter and deafening silence . . . my mind is somewhere else . . . help me . . . I'm slipping . . . twenty-five years in prison . . . the faces around me have no features . . . the fog settles . . . dizzy . . . weak . . . losing it, man . . . swimming . . . what have I done . . . hands settle upon me . . . I feel the metal of the cuffs . . . my body is limp and my strength sapped . . . the air feels so heavy . . . I can't draw a breath . . . faint voices echo in the recesses of my mind . . . murder . . . can't be . . . who cares what they say? . . . I killed a man . . . he's gone from this world forever . . . I had no right . . . why . . . why . . . footsteps . . . hollow and deep corridors . . . the jangle of keys . . . walls all around me and a smell of stale urine . . . faces . . . all these faces . . . don't look at me . . . what have I done . . . he can't be dead . . . tragic . . . fatal . . . final . . . God gives life and no man has the right to take it . . . there's nothing left . . . hell closes its door on me . . . unreal . . . this is just a dream . . . a vicious nightmare . . .

My fury subsides as the water drips from my naked flesh. Drops of water dripping . . . dripping away the fury and resentment seizing my entire being.

The bastards went too far this time. They have just nailed another spike in their coffin. How can they get away with this brutality? How do they justify it? They're barbaric and sadistic clones. That's the only possible answer . . . the only reason for their insanity.

They take delight in administering their brand of correction and corruption. They think they're impervious to swift and lethal justice . . . Oh, no, I've had enough of this bullshit . . . no more from anyone.

17

I'll Get Mine

Damp, cold and suffocating. The screws and their senseless brutality and torments. Their day is drawing near. Keep driving, because nothing breaks this guy. Wait till I get you in *my* dungeon.

I'm shivering . . . freezing. I can't let anyone else suffer like this . . . I need that paper and pencil. I have to write a letter confessing I'm the culprit who started the fire in the yard last week. The other guys had nothing to do with it. I'll take the rap and you'll have to let them go. I may not like the guys very much, but I can spare them this hellish treatment. I don't wish this shit on anyone . . . anyone but those who mete it out.

That damn fire and soot made it difficult to breathe. The fiberglass burned like an inferno. That was an adrenaline rush. It's a good thing the guys hollered long and hard enough for the screws to get us out on time; we could have been asphyxiated. Flakes of black soot fell from the air like volcanic ash.

There are times when breathing is difficult down here in the hole too. Is it hyperventilation, as the mad doctor says, or are you poisoning me? At times, I swear I'm going to die because I can't take a full breath. Could you kill me and make it look like an accident? I know the crazed doctor would cover up a murderous plot with his autopsy. He's on my hit list, the prick.

I've had plenty of experience with these mad medical men in these joints. They're just glorified dope pushers. They have violated their sacred oath. Where are their ethics? Yes ... you demented doctors will be made to pay ...

Wacko warden, 1981

Walking shakily toward the bars of the prison cell-block, I encounter a short, bespectacled doctor who hands me a Dixie cup full of medication. He says this will keep me calm and help me sleep. I nod and then swallow the various pills. There must have been more than ten of them in that small paper container.

Moments pass, then the sleeping pills begin to make me feel drowsy. I can barely keep my eyes open as the anxiety in the pit of my stomach goes to numb. Blackness comes and I drift into oblivion . . .

I awaken from my slumber and wonder how long

I've been sleeping. Standing unsteadily, I wobble to my cell door and am surprised to see it's broad daylight. Lifting the small steel latch on my door, I swing it open. As I walk into the bright and empty range, I sense I must have slept a very long time. I'm famished.

Making my way to the end of the range, I call out to the screw on duty. A fat screw with thick glasses approaches and I ask him how long I've been sleeping. Three days, he says, and goes on to ask if I'd like to see the doctor again.

I struggle to remember what's happened in the last four months, but my mind draws a blank. What was everyone saying after the verdict was read? I knew first-degree murder meant I was facing a minimum of twenty-five years, and in some very tough prisons.

I killed someone . . .

I'm sure I had a bail hearing, but I don't remember being there. I'm in a state of severe shock. Why am I alone on a range capable of holding twenty men? I'm caged up like a wild animal. What have I done to deserve such treatment? Yes, I've killed someone, but it was a tragic accident. It WAS an accident.

These good-for-nothing barbarians know I would never kill someone on purpose. The police and Crown must have given them some information about the murder. The screws know me in this shit-house. They know I'm not a damned killer.

I might like to cause a few problems in jail, but I won't do so with such a serious charge. I don't need anyone saying I'm violent. They know this. They hate me and they like to power-trip. They are pun-ishing me for things I did in the past. Jerks, I already paid the price for those Mickey Mouse charges and I don't think it's fair to have to pay twice for the same thing. This is bullshit.

My mind still foggy, I ask the screw why I'm alone on the range and he says he doesn't know. Have I done anything wrong in the last few months, I ask? He tells me I haven't done anything wrong in the last four months. Now I'm baffled and begin to suspect the warden is harboring a hatred for me.

Who does he think he is? Do you assholes think you can keep me stoned and half-conscious for another six months? I don't think so. To hell with it. I'll accost the warden during his regular rounds. The stupid warden loves to walk around his jail like some arrogant big shot. I know he can't resist these ego boosters. It gives him a sense of power and control over those in captivity . . .

Sure enough, early one morning the predictable warden, cloaked in his air of importance, struts proudly outside the range that I'm in. Flanked by two burly screws, he stops abruptly and peers contemptuously through the bars. The idiot is trying to play the mob boss or something.

Trying to ignore his contempt, I ask if he'd consider placing a few inmates on the range with me, because, frankly, I don't understand why I should be kept alone on a range capable of holding twenty men.

Raising thick eyebrows, his neck slightly crooked, the warden casts a victorious glance at his cronies. The smug-looking screws seem to be enjoying his sense of power and control. He remarks sharply through disdainful lips that the only company I'll keep will be the company of my conscience—in solitary confinement.

The asshole goes on to say I've already killed a man and will probably do it again. Then he turns and walks away abruptly, with his two flunkies close behind.

That rat bastard is power-tripping. Cursing him under my breath, I start thinking about ways to get him. I'm at his mercy and see no way to escape. I'm enraged. I've been alone for four months already and have five more to wait before my trial will begin. I'll go insane for sure if I'm not allowed to be around other people.

A few days after my words with the warden, I receive a visit from my older brother Mike, who sees I'm visibly shaken by the warden's head games. My brother proposes a great way to deal with the tyrant. Gesturing through the thick Plexiglas partition in the visiting area, Mike mimes an idea that will soften him up.

I figure the no-good son of a bitch will have to be taught a lesson. Nobody, but nobody messes with me, and nobody power-trips without incurring my revenge. Who the hell does he think he is, carrying out a personal vendetta in this prison? Is he above the law? We know how to break a few of our own. He'll be made to pay, and pay dearly.

He'll be humbled, the rat. He'll come to realize that you can't push a man too far and expect to go unpunished. The name is Dubé and don't you forget it. The whole jail will be made to pay for the warden's insolence and their quiet collaboration.

My brother will go out late tonight and put dynamite under the warden's car. He'll ignite the fuse and the warden's brand-new car will be blown up right in his driveway. Then my brother will drive by the prison and throw a stick of dynamite into the front yard to signal the job is complete.

I figure this ought to send these monsters a pretty good message. And if that doesn't soften them up, their porches, garages and boats will come next. I hope they listen at this point, because more is to follow. Property first, but people come next.

I return to my empty range after the visit with my

brother and spend the day pacing anxiously. I know now there's light at the end of the tunnel. I look at the screws and see their last arrogant looks. I think about what the warden will soon feel like. He should have listened to me and he shouldn't be so hard and insensitive. The jerk has no idea what he's doing or who he's messing with.

I'm relieved when the night finally arrives. Lying on my small bunk, I wait patiently for the roar of a dynamite blast that will signal revenge and my last day alone on this long and empty range.

Around midnight, lying quietly on my bunk, I feel the foundation of the jail tremble. Sitting up on my cot, I listen as the steel-barred doors of my cage rattle. As I put my naked feet on the cold hard floor, the tremors flow throughout my whole body. I swear an earthquake has struck. Such is the power of the dynamite blast in the prison yard. The warden must have shit his pants by now.

Closing my eyes, I lie back down on my small cot as a huge smile cuts across my face. The sound and effect was much more powerful than I could ever have dreamed. I'm sure the screws spilled their coffee when the blast rocked the jail. The inmates are awake from the shock.

The jerks have no idea what's just happened. The screws are murmuring, and many believe the miners who've been blasting underground must have caused the powerful explosion. Idiots. The mines have never made such severe tremors travel down the halls of this putrid hellhole.

I gather my flannel blanket around my body. I sleep soundly, satisfied that the warden has received his message in a bomb. I wonder what the idiot is thinking now . . .

The loud banging of countless doors and an extraordinary hustle and bustle announce the arrival of morning. I badly want to see the warden. I will select my words carefully. The idiot probably didn't sleep very well and I can't wait to see his bloodshot eyes.

I tell the screw on duty to get me down to the warden's office right away. Burning my eyes into his, I wonder if he knows . . .

I am not surprised when the warden is quick to respond to my demand to see him this morning. The atmosphere in his stinking jail is unlike all the other dull and boring days. I see nervousness and confusion pasted on everyone's face and there's a real stir going on. The place is alive; there are vibes shooting through these concrete slabs for a change. There's a tension in the air—and I love it. Even the cons are more excited than usual, and it's obvious the administration is very anxious. I can smell the tension and fear. This is DYNAMITE.

Walking into the warden's office, complete with

handcuffs and escort, I smile broadly as I observe the extra security on hand. I'm delighted to see the main man. Sitting behind his large desk, his face is sullen and withdrawn. The bastard is not his usual arrogant self this morning. His ego has been stomped on pretty bad.

The warden has a full house in his office this morning. Four burly screws, the assistant warden and he and I are crammed into his small office.

Standing quietly, I look him straight in the eye. I try to silently communicate that I know of his plight. Can he read my eyes? Let me smile a little. There, that's better. He looks pretty tight-lipped today. Good. He knows.

Breaking the tense silence, the warden asks why I've chosen to see him today. Now I'll tell him and humble the rat.

I assume an exaggerated air of arrogance like his, look intently into his bulging eyes, demand four guys on my range by sundown, and go on to name them. I see shock and fear in his face as I tell him what I want. The prick recoils and I swear I can smell his cowardice.

Looking around the office, I stare every screw in the face, trying to communicate the message that they're next if they dare to say or do anything stupid. These idiots too are immobile and paralyzed.

I'm serious and I have a crazed look in my eyes.

My top lip is curled as a look of hatred burns forth from my face. I glare at them with contempt.

Gathering his thoughts and straightening himself in his seat, the warden leans over on his desk and asks me again why I've decided to see him this morning and make such a specific request. What a jerk. Does he think I'm going to confess?

In response to his stupid question, I merely lean slowly over and peer into his twisted face. Then I smile broadly, wink and turn to leave his office.

As these impressions dance in his mind, I'm escorted out of his office and returned to my range.

By sundown, I have the four men I have asked for . . . but is this more of the warden's game to set me up?

I wouldn't be in this dark abyss of misery and torture if it weren't for that corrupt and sick warden back home. He's at the top of my hit list. My food slot opens, a brown paper bag is shoved inside and lands on the wet floor . . .

They're huddled in the corner, trying to keep warm with their body heat . . . you want heat, I'll give you heat . . . pouring hot water down the pit, I throw an electrical cord in the pool . . . their bodies stiffen . . . electrical currents pass through their jiggling carcasses . . . they're frying . . .

18

Eviction Notice

A screw with thick shoulders and a black handlebar moustache shows up at my door and advises me in a monotone that I've served my time in the hole. He quickly reminds me of the six pending charges I face. I have to be moved to segregation to wait for the next session of kangaroo court. Sorry, but I'm not moving out of my home. I've grown accustomed to this cave.

The burly screw shakes his big head and grimaces. He doesn't look very pleased. Exasperated, he goes on to say they need the room for other cases. No way; I'll spare my brothers in arms this hellish experience. I'm a noble savage, remember?

The screw leaves with a heavy sigh and I begin to wonder what they'll do. They don't understand why I don't want to leave the hole. Most guys jump at the chance, but I've reached a point where I've accepted that I'll do the rest of my time in the hole, even if they gate me. That would be a total of eighteen more months.

Moments later, the shrink comes to my cell. He peers through my food slot and watches me as I lie quietly on my steel cot. I'm stark naked, unshaven, and I don't care what he thinks. I'm not saying a single word to that crackpot.

The shrink is expressionless and tries to read me. Want in my head, doorknob? You'll be terrified to read me, asshole. Don't you know I want to kill you? Look at what they're doing. How does this sit with your schooling and psychology texts? Is what you're doing to me rational and sane? This place would turn anyone into a raving maniac.

The nut looks away and I know they want to take me out of the hole. They're becoming afraid of what they've created. They can't handle it anymore. The doors are going to open wide in a few days. Where will you hide? Where will you go when I come for you?

The door to my dungeon slides open and clothes are set in front of my door. When did they mop the area? I must have slept for a few minutes. These assholes can be quiet when they want to.

I slide off my hard cot and decide to throw on some warm clean clothes. I'm still cold and shivering. I'm going to segregation? Should I go? Maybe a little break will do me good.

The clothes feel good . . . I'm almost polished. I wonder what I look like. I haven't seen my reflection in many weeks. Feeling my chin, I feel the hair. I wonder if it's gray and dirty . . . I don't like to see my reflection anyway. I look so . . . so . . . different these days.

Is that little mouthpiece looking at me? I see his eyes in the crack of the door. Take a good look at me, kid, because I'm your worst nightmare. Do you see the ripples of the muscles in my gut? Can you see the lines across my pectorals? Even my shoulders are ripped and striated. Yet these are only a manifestation of the burning fury inside. My strength isn't physical, it's psychological. I feel no pain and have no fear. I'm fast and I hit very hard.

I know some of the cons find the time very long down here, but to me it's like my second home. I use it to get away from all of you. I don't like you, but I'm solid. I'm on short time and you have respected and feared me for years. I'm not bluffing anymore. Do your time and I'll do mine.

I always grant you respect and I'm always honest. I don't take any of your bullshit and trips. I was taught the codes and I live by them religiously.

I'm being led down the narrow corridor past the door to the kangaroo court. Turning right, we head toward the door leading to segregation. I wonder who's locked up in segregation today. The door swings open and we walk by long rows of cells. I feel the eyes on me, but nobody utters a word.

Stopping abruptly, the screw motions for the screw in the bubble to crack open my new home. The door hums silently and I hesitate. Should I refuse again or should I stay? It would take a lot of effort to get me back to the hole.

I'll stay a few days and think of something to do. I'll have regular showers, once every two days, yard exercise for half an hour a day and even a radio. I have a blanket, pillow and mattress. This is luxury down below in the big house. If they're on good behavior, some cons even have televisions. I'll never get one.

I step into my cell and check the water faucet. Holy shit, cool running water. I flush my toilet and the damn thing works. Water, mattress, pillow, yard, clothes and showers. This is pretty good. I can even get some paper and pens. I must write that letter for the guys in the hole. They'll be let out once I do this, even the little mouthpiece. If he feels brave enough, maybe he'll come to segregation. What will I do then? The parole hearing must be scheduled to take place soon. I better call a damn lawyer.

But I have to address a problem down here first. Lots on my damn mind. Too much. The guys in segregation are giving Lorne a hard time. A few are threatening to kill him.

I met Lorne in population a few months ago. As neighbors on the same range, we spoke frequently. He is one of the few cons I allowed in my cell for rap sessions. I like him because he seems honest and open. A quiet guy, he does his own time and doesn't bother anybody.

Guys like him are not suited for this madhouse. He comes from a good home with good values. His parents are well-off, but he got lazy and tried to cut corners. The guy didn't want to work or go to school, so he sold dope. He's just a dope pusher and a party animal. He got in with the wrong crowd on the street and again in here, and he can't adapt to this environment. There a few like him around here. They usually get taken out on a stretcher. Or die.

He's not very big at five-nine. Weighing in at 165 pounds, he certainly doesn't look like he can defend himself. His innocent features have not been darkened by the kill or be killed mentality. Timid and reserved, he's the perfect target. A loner with no desire to kill and take it to the limit is prime prey around here. He's also a short-timer and a little naïve sometimes. He has a dope conviction but no violence on his rap sheet, and thinks this place is like the subculture on the streets. He's sadly mistaken.

They are calling Lorne a goof and a rat. These two words have caused many men to die in here . . .

Dead time, 1981

My trial is scheduled to begin in a few months and it doesn't look very good, despite the fact that at my preliminary hearing, my first-degree murder charge was reduced to second-degree. I'm now facing life, with eligibility for parole after a minimum of ten years instead of twenty-five. Not exactly a godsend. Life in prison is a difficult prospect to face, no matter if it's second- or first-degree murder. The whole ordeal is a nightmare.

I feel a part of myself being swallowed by the system, with its many games and its special mentality. But I desperately want to remain free.

Another big question remains at the forefront of my mind: I want to suffer for what I did—but how much?

I work out an escape plan. Everything is coming to a head and the pressures mount daily. I decide there's no way I could serve a ten- to fourteen-year sentence locked up like an animal. I'm prepared to accept five to seven years, and perhaps a flat ten-year sentence, but not life in prison. I can't imagine being locked up for such a long time. I'm only twenty years old. Killing is horrible, but it was an accident. I didn't mean to kill this man. It was a horrible and tragic mistake.

The thought of escaping develops into a full-fledged plan. The plot is simple and sure to shake the foundation of the prison. It's so novel and daring it will catch the prison officials with their pants down. I'll escape from the most secure place the jail has to offer. Solitary confinement. My plan is laid out and I'll carry it out if I get a life sentence.

When I'm convicted of second-degree murder, I'll demand to be placed in solitary confinement. I'll say I need quiet time. My request will be honored in light of the fear the prison's administrators feel at this point.

The cells in solitary confinement have a loophole in their security devices. The ceiling in one of the cells has a six- by four-foot opening, fortified with a quarter-inch steel screen, which is covered with a plastic dome. There's a camera in the hole, but it presents no real problem. I could either break the camera facing my cell or cover it with my prison garb, explaining that I want to grieve unobserved. Or I could toss a wet wad of toilet paper at the eye of the camera, as I've done many times before.

Being in the hole, I'll be in an excellent position to escape with some outside help—which I have. My older brother Mike has agreed to assist me in my time of need if the conviction proves too hard to bear. He'll climb to the roof of the prison with rope, lock cutters and a gun. He'll cut through the plastic dome, remove the steel grate and drop the rope down to me. He'll leave the gun on the roof and park a stolen vehicle a few blocks down the street. An apartment will be rented for two months and fully stocked with enough goods to last until the heat cools off and a large collection of disguises.

I have no doubt in my mind that if anyone tries to stop me, I'll put a few bullets in their legs. I'm willing to die, rather than go to prison for life.

Days roll into weeks and weeks into months as the dreaded trial date nears. The charge is still second-degree murder and I'm not optimistic of having it reduced to manslaughter. Everything looks dim. Merle Haggard puts out his smash hit song with the line "I turned twenty-one in prison doin' life without parole."

Too bad Lorne can't escape this hellhole, because the cons want his blood. These thirsting psychos need very little reason to bludgeon him to death. And he's so damn naïve. He can't trust anybody, but I wonder if he'll trust me.

The boys in blue are the visible enemy, but he can't see the others so well. I wonder if Lorne is aware of the old adage that goes "God save me from my friends, as I can take care of my enemies on my own." In here, his very life depends on his aware-ness. Violence and intelligence are this life's companions.

19

Lawyers' Games

Lorne is about to be killed. I know it. Why hasn't anyone taught him the law of the land?

Why are the guys in here so patently stupid? They talk about codes, but who can live by them? I know what's right and wrong in here. I know the cleavage line. You don't label some guy a rat or a goof without some kind of proof, or you'll end up dead. Can't these guys see they're threatening Lorne's very life with their murderous rumors? I've seen the casualties around here.

The smashed body lay on the cold hard floor for several hours. The prisoners milled about, oblivious to it. The screws in their turrets didn't see it.

I witnessed the vicious attack. There were only four of us in the gym that morning: two assailants, the victim and myself. A six-foot steel bar used for weightlifting was used as a club that was swung with lethal force. The second attacker picked up another weightlifting bar as the victim sprawled unconscious on the floor and hit him twice. Then the thugs left quickly. I sat nearby in shock and horror. What had I just seen? I ran out and caught up with one of the thugs.

He walked around the yard for several minutes, telling me the idiot had it coming. I said nothing in reply. He had to know I would never tell the authorities. I would never tell a soul.

We sit in this madhouse and the new cons we call "fish" don't know what to expect. Many tough and hardened cons wait for the day when they can show the fish what the codes are.

We can never complain, nor ask any questions at all, and never ever show fear. We can never back down from a fight or point a finger. Never whistle. Never utter friendly words to the screws or leave your cell to speak to the police. Never go into protective custody. Don't sit in anyone else's chair. Don't change channels on the television set unless you're ready to fight.

Don't put your nose into anybody's affairs. You see nothing, hear nothing and say nothing. Don't shed tears. Don't talk about rehabilitation. Never cheat at cards. Do what you say you'll do. Stay quiet and respect the others. Keep yourself fit and stay alert.

Don't peer into other people's cells. Never receive gifts from others. Don't gossip. Don't ask for anything from anyone. Know your surroundings and the players through observation and listening. Don't be part of any cliques. Never fully reveal your emotions or potential for survival.

I survive because my would-be assailants never know how far I'm willing to go if a fight ever breaks out. Some witnessed my fury from a distance and decided it wasn't worth taking a chance with me. In many cases I was lucky, and I'm certain of that. I communicate well at their level and know how to read people. I stay by myself and try to respect everyone. However, respect is not always recipro- cated. I know what to do in that case also: kill or be killed.

My assailants aren't sure they can beat me. They figure they'll have to kill me so I won't retaliate. But they'd need a very good reason for killing me, wouldn't they? Not really. They only need to be sure they won't be killed themselves if they try.

Their reasons for killing vary according to their values and beliefs. But most need very little reason to kill. Hurt pride and a bad word have been known to cause severe bloodletting.

I've seen the games from both sides of the fence. Life has no value. It's all based on revenge, retribu- tion and punishment . . .

Deal-making, 1981

In their usual cold plea-bargaining process, the lawyer and Crown attorney are trying to determine how long I should serve in jail, based on what they perceive to be the value of my victim's life. It's an inhumane process.

As for myself, I understand I have to pay for what I've done, but I won't pay for something the law says I didn't do. I certainly didn't intend to kill anyone. So how could the lawyers say a ten- or seven-year sentence is worth the life of another? I could serve a hundred years and never make book for that tragedy. I could never make up for what I did, no matter how long I serve in jail or how severe the punishment.

I fire my first one and set my sights on out-of-town lawyers. I've read the statutes and I know I fit the criteria for manslaughter. But my search for a lawyer meets with severe opposition from the legal aid office. I'm told legal aid won't pay for an out-of-town lawyer and I'll have to find a lawyer here in Sudbury to handle my case.

I don't feel I can get fair and just representation from a local lawyer because they tend to exchange favors with the Crown's office. I could be sold out and counted on as a favor later. I won't be rail-roaded. With my trial fast approaching, the pressure mounts. I become extremely agitated. I feel cornered and very anxious. What can I do?

With no other recourse, I tell the director of legal aid that the police will have to drag me into court if they won't honor my request to fund an out-of-town lawyer. I'll scream and fight all the way. I'll disrupt the proceedings and will have to be ejected from the courtroom. I'll holler that a travesty of justice is being perpetrated and that I'm being sold out. I'll lash out at anyone I can reach.

I'll also request a change of venue and a motion to have my trial held in French. I'll use up taxpayers' dollars and scream injustice all the way. The media will have a field day with my antics—and I'll look at an insanity plea as well.

In light of my threats, the director accepts my wishes and nothing more is said about the selection of my lawyer. I feel my constitutional rights have been respected and not compromised over fiscal considerations. I also believe I've avoided a diabolical plan hatched by local lawyers to sell me out.

Moreover, I could abandon my plan to escape. Why should I escape via violence if I can escape via intelligence?

With this victory, I begin to call the biggest names in the legal profession, but none will accept what legal aid pays. Many days and countless calls later, I'm referred to a lawyer in London, Ontario, who's handled a case for a guy currently locked up in the

Sudbury jail. The lawyer did a good job of pleading the case, so I want an opportunity to size him up. This lawyer agrees to see me.

When Fletcher Dawson arrives, I see my man is young, eager and intelligent. Short blond hair crowns a thin face and long jawline. I look into his clear blue eyes and sense immediately that I can trust him. He tells me my options are wide open. I like that.

We discuss the case briefly and he indicates he'll come back to see me soon. The trial is scheduled to begin in a month and a half.

Two weeks pass and my lawyer returns with the assurance he can get me a seven-year sentence on a manslaughter conviction. I figure he's doing a fine job, since this means a possible release after fourteen months on good behavior.

Encouraged, I decide to bargain a little more and tell him to ask the Crown attorney for a three-year deal in return for pleading guilty. The young attorney is doubtful and leaves shaking his head in exasperation. When he returns a week later, he has an offer of five years on the table. The game is on.

A five-year sentence means parole after ten months if I receive a full parole. Not bad, but I want three years. I sense the Crown has a weak case if he's willing to offer such a deal.

Two weeks later, and about three weeks before

my trial is scheduled to begin, my lawyer advises me
to either accept the five-year deal or be tried for
second-degree murder. I tell him I'll take a week to
think about it . . .

Cursing and issuing threats, the guys in segregation are asking Lorne to come out in the yard and
clear his name. These guys are after blood. They
want him bad. But does anyone have any proof of
their allegations? I don't think they do, so they
better shut their fat traps. Nobody gets to Lorne but
through me. It is against prison codes to label somebody without proof. Cons who label others falsely
are killed.

I know some of these guys have killed before, but
what am I going to do? I can't let them label Lorne a
goof and a rat without proof. Enough is enough. I'll
teach these psychos the codes. I'll fight them if they
give me no choice. Two hundred and fifty pounds of
muscle is nothing to me if they can't use it wisely.
Furthermore, I'm following the codes, but these
guys are being immature and exhibiting the mentality of reformatory boys. This is Millhaven and it has
a mentality of its own.

Yelling through my cell door down the length of
the range, I tell Lorne not to worry, nobody is going
to touch him in the yard. He has the right to tell his
side of the story and I want to hear it.

I hear mumbling and ask who it is. It's the big gun from the special-handling unit. He and his murderous partner are fuelling the cons. The SHU has a reputation, but nobody rides on reputation alone in here. They better adhere to the codes—or die by them.

I've had enough of this shithouse and the duplicity from both sides. I know their true colors. They pick on the weak like a pack of wolves. They need to satisfy their thirst for blood. They know how to pick their targets. Lorne certainly can't retaliate and it seems he has no friends.

Fuck that, man. When's the last time they fought head to head without weapons, without sneaking behind someone like cowards? Anybody can stick a dirty knife in another's back, but how many can kill with their bare hands in a face-to-face battle?

I call down the length of the narrow range; I tell Lorne to come out to the yard and talk to me. If he lies to me, I'll take him out. I won't need anybody's help and he knows that. I assure him nobody will come near him if he comes out. If he's innocent, he'll come out.

Lorne says he doesn't trust anybody anymore. Good, he's doing very well—but what about principle? Deathly silence follows . . .

Peering into the makeshift prison, I toss a cup of acid on the fat copper's hairy back. Sitting bolt upright, shock registered on his fat bulbous face, the purple veins of his alcoholic nose are about to burst. Smoke begins to smolder as he chokes in excruciating pain. What a blast. Screw him and his slinking ilk.

You should have never punked me off. This is nothing. Wait till I take you and your friends out for a car ride later. Boy, are you going to suffer with that trip.

The judge is shuffling around like a damn walrus. Maybe I should take him out and give him a few good shots in the face. Crack his nose and break his filthy jaw.

I can feel the hate burning my stomach as it rests in my gut like a football. It rises to my throat and spews forth like a damn volcano. I feel like a raving lunatic — a tornado. Being mad isn't such a bad trip. It's actually a lot of fun.

20

Judgment Call

Silence. Everyone is silent and I know Lorne is struggling with the thought of trusting me. The big guns from the SHU are quiet now. They know Lorne is no longer alone. But the word is out and Lorne will never survive when I leave. The only chance he has is to come out to the yard and confront his accusers. I'm willing to back him up. I'm putting my neck out for him. He better come out now, or I'll find a way to get him.

I'm not like the rest of the guys down here. I have to have proof; I give a man the benefit of the doubt before pronouncing him guilty. The nuts in here are just like the system they hate. The presumption of innocence is invalid.

As I pace, my anger mounts. I've never seen these loudmouths, but I've heard of them. They stabbed a guy—killed him—for some stupid reason. They like to kill. But I'm sure they don't like being hurt. They've seen what happens when a man squirms and flinches on the ground. That could very well happen to them. I'm not afraid of these damn loud-mouths.

I better stretch and limber up a little. Loosen up the neck muscles and get ready to roll with the punches. I'm going to kick, hit, bite, tear and poke . . .

Judgment, 1982

Cuffed, I'm escorted to the courthouse through the subterranean tunnel and placed in the prisoner's box I occupied eight months ago. Only this time, I'm not facing twenty-five years, but twenty-five months.

A lot of people have come to court to hear my sentencing. The press has been unusually quiet about the proceedings, but some people have taken an interest in the case. There's a classroom of young students present and a number of other people, including my family.

As for myself, I feel reasonably sure I'll get the five-year deal and be transferred to a minimum-security penitentiary, where I'll probably be released on parole in twenty months.

The court clerk announces the judge's entrance. The play is about to unfold. All the actors have read their scripts and I hope nobody forgets their lines. The lead player, the judge begins to speak . . .

"The accused has been charged with the offense of second-degree murder as a result of the death of one _____ on or about the 13th day of May, 1981, at the city of Sudbury.

"On arraignment, the accused pleaded not guilty to the offense as charged, namely second-degree murder, but tendered a plea of guilty to the included offense of manslaughter. The Crown consented to the acceptance of this plea to the lesser offense of manslaughter.

"The accused met the deceased, _____, at the Coulson Hotel in the city of Sudbury at approximately 8 p.m. of the night in question. The accused was present with the deceased until approximately midnight, during which period of time they were obviously consuming alcoholic beverages. The deceased, at some time near or about midnight, went to the registration desk of the hotel and rented a room, apparently in his name, following which the deceased and the accused went to that room.

"The cause of death as given by the pathologist at the autopsy was edema secondary to traumatic head injuries.

"He also states that a contributing cause of death was the acute alcoholic intoxication of the deceased at the time of his death.

"The Crown gave brief reasons for consenting to the acceptance of the plea of guilty to manslaughter,

with which reasons I entirely agree. There is substantial evidence that the deceased was robbed at
some time, but the evidence is not conclusive that
the accused was the perpetrator of the robbery. The
evidence of robbery appeared in the turned-out
lining of the pockets of the deceased, the folder of
his wallet lying on the bed and the absence of any
money, as I understand the evidence. In any event,
I'm perfectly satisfied that there's no way in which
the Crown could have proven beyond a reasonable
doubt that this accused robbed the deceased, or that
robbery was in any way the motivation on the part
of the accused for this death of the deceased. It was
on the basis of the consumption of alcohol and the
evidence of provocation, which the jury would have
to very carefully consider, that I decided that the
appropriate offense was manslaughter and not
second-degree murder, and I therefore entered a
conviction against this accused for the offense of
manslaughter. The maximum penalty to which the
accused is liable for manslaughter is imprisonment
for life.

"I now turn to some of the matters that I must
take into account in determining what is the appropriate sentence for this offense of manslaughter.

"The accused was born August 3, 1960, so that he
was twenty years of age at the time of this offense
and he's now twenty-one years of age. He has been

in custody since May 13, 1981, which is a period of almost eight months. This period of pretrial confinement must of course be taken into account in determining what is an appropriate sentence. The fact that the accused has entered a plea of guilty to the offense of manslaughter has thereby obviated the necessity of a trial and is also a factor to be taken into account in his favor. On the other hand, the accused has been convicted of ten offenses, exclusive of this conviction for manslaughter, between December 29, 1976, at which time he was just slightly over the age of sixteen years, and March 25, 1981, at which time he was twenty years of age.

"Just summarizing very briefly the nature of those convictions, they included a conviction for fraud, mischief to private property, causing a disturbance, trafficking in a controlled drug, assault occasioning bodily harm, a breach of recognizance causing a disturbance, and failure to appear, causing a disturbance, assault occasioning bodily harm and theft over $200. No one of those convictions alone is of an extremely serious nature, but taken as a whole they indicate a complete disregard of the law by this accused and a lifestyle that was bound to lead to something very serious, as he now has encountered.

"The report of Doctor Racinskas, which has been filed as exhibit 4 in these proceedings, provides what I perceive to be a proper assessment of this accused when he reports as follows:

"'Personality testing reveals him to have a character disorder. He's likely to be seen as lacking insight into his own motivations, egocentric, shallow and as having difficulty forming meaningful long-term relationships. Such persons typically show a lack of deep emotional response, inability to profit from past experience, inability to plan ahead and a reckless disregard for the consequences of their behavior. The lack of social conformity and a persistent tendency to get into difficulties with the law are characteristic, along with a history of alcohol abuse and sexual acting out. Such individuals demonstrate an unusually high threshold and tolerance for punishment, such that punitive measures have negligible impact in redirecting their behavior. He's quite likely to make a good initial impression, but the moodiness and resentment is likely to undo that impression over time.

"'There was no evidence of psychosis nor strong aggressive or hostile themes that would suggest that he's dangerous.

"'It appears, then, that in the incident in question, his degree of impairment by alcohol, combined with a typical poor evaluation for the consequences of his behavior, led to his beating the man more than he had anticipated.

"'As you know, traditional psychiatric intervention with such individuals has been extremely disappointing, and one could therefore anticipate that he similarly would gain little benefit. A fundamental impediment to such intervention is that it would be extremely difficult, if not impossible, to form a trusting psychotherapeutic relationship with him. A structured rehabilitation environment would seem to be the best course of action.'

"In summary, I must on the one hand take into account the youth of the accused, his plea of guilty and the time he has already spent in custody. On the other hand, I must keep in mind that the fundamental purpose of sentencing is the protection of society. To that end, the sentence that I impose should act especially as a deterrent to this accused and at the same time provide a structured rehabilitation environment for him. Penal sanctions in the past have not been effective in altering the conduct of this accused and one can only hope that this further opportunity for rehabilitation of the accused will bear fruit. It's entirely up to the accused and no one else whether or not that proves to be the case.

"Both counsel for the Crown and the accused have suggested the appropriate penalty for this accused for this offense is a term of imprisonment for five years. Although I always appreciate the assistance of counsel in this regard, I of course am not bound in any way by their views.

"In this case, however, I believe that a sentence of five years is the appropriate sentence, and I therefore impose it as a result of my own consideration of all the factors which I am in law bound to consider. The sentence of the Court is therefore imprisonment for five years.

"I may say that I would think that the parole authorities, if they are to consider a mitigation or lessening of the sentence of this accused, would want to be looking for a very substantial and persuasive change in attitude and conduct on his part during his term of confinement. It's often said that individuals are at the crossroads in their lives. I wouldn't think that there is a more glaring example of a person who is in that position than this accused today. Should he ever return to Court with a conviction for a very serious offense, there would really be very little that could be said on his behalf to mitigate the results of his conduct.

"I should also state in conclusion that both counsel for the accused and for the Crown have stated to me that they don't believe that a presentence report would be of any assistance to me. Having listened very carefully to the evidence and the very able submissions of counsel for the Crown and for the accused, I agree with those views.

Mr. Dubé, I may say, sir, that you have been very well represented in these proceedings, and if you don't understand and appreciate that, the next time that you stand up and have to look a judge in the eye, I don't think he will be as considerate as I have been of your situation today . . . "

Tell me, Doc, what do you think about sharing your personal experience of hell? You haven't been able to up to this point, have you? Perhaps you'll be able to identify with your client base now. Born with a silver spoon in your mouth, were you? Come from a good home, do you? Healthy family dynamics and the material benefits as well? Discipline at home, and good values instilled? Yes? Tools to render wise decisions and all? Avoided alcohol and other pitfalls? Such as drugs? Was it luck or wisdom, asshole? Don't talk to me about your infamous evaluation criteria, jerkoff . . . trying to stereotype me again. Would you say I'm detaching from reality as a defense mechanism now? Who wouldn't in such sickly dynamics? I don't have my drugs to detach right now? You'd rather pump me full of pills because we can't connect our fields of experience . . . you have failed to keep yourself objective because of your value judgments on me . . . you're afraid . . . you don't care why I do what I do. I'm a societal writeoff in your biased eyes . . . you prefer to keep me locked up . . . you fail to intervene. Your own inade-

*quacy breeds this insane seeding ground. You're part
of the problem . . . . Blame me, do you? You're a sick
bastard . . .*

*Take this bug juice . . . it should help you sleep
better . . . you'll feel better in the morning . . . just
numb out some more. I want you to write me a 25,000-
word essay on the pros and cons of intervention and
create a model for primary, secondary and tertiary
intervention for ex-cons. Re-evaluate your own
approach and take a good look at yourself . . . give
your profession a whole new perspective . . . . What's
the best way to intervene and to help? Is incarceration
a panacea? Take another look at where you are, idiot.
I think you're in denial . . .*

The cell doors open wide and the guys are led to
an enclosure ringed by a twenty-foot barbed wire
fence. A single tower looks down on the forty- by
twenty-five-foot yard. About ten guys mill about
casually. Lorne has come outside. He looks very
nervous.

I stride over to Lorne's side and he tells me he's
been ripped off. He was dealing drugs in this hellhole. Bad move. Too many killings revolve around
drugs in here.

Lorne says he had some cash brought through the
visiting room by one of his visitors and stuffed the
bundle up his ass. He gave the money to another

con, who'd done the same with some drugs. But the drugs never got to Lorne.

The guys responsible for the ripoff had written a letter to the administration saying Lorne's life was in danger. The administration then locked him up in segregation for his own protection.

I'm pumped. The guys in population had started this rumor that could get an innocent man killed. Shit. Word travels very fast and very far in this small community. The kid won't be safe anywhere until the issue is resolved. He has to get back to population and get those guys, but the administration won't let him out of segregation. He's in a catch-22. He's on short time as well, which doesn't help his cause. The guys know how to pick their targets. They're crazy, but they're not stupid. The most dangerous guys are the ones who have a combination of intelligence and violence.

I see the psychos from the SHU lurking and observing us. I feel their eyes burn my back. I know I'm the only thing between Lorne and the thugs.

Mike and Sammy, in the far corner of the yard, are going to the SHU because they bludgeoned a guy to death a few months ago. They want Lorne's ass and they're friendly with his enemies. Lorne is trapped. They're fuelling the masses and looking for some justification and support to kill Lorne without incurring a backlash.

Lorne is petrified. His paranoid blue eyes search the yard. Loosening the zipper on his green jacket, he says he's ready to tackle anyone who sticks their nose in his business. Pulling a cigarette from his right jacket pocket, he lights up and draws on it. The kid has no clue what he's talking about. Nobody is going to just come up and slug it out. In fact, they could pull out some hardware any minute and start bludgeoning us to death.

Beware, Lorne; this isn't some reformatory or rock 'n' roll tavern back home. I know these guys want to drive it right through you. How do I know that? Because you're thinking violence. Rubbing a tattooed hand over his stubbly chin, Lorne wonders what he can do now.

21

Protect the Weak

I look away from Lorne and scan the menacing faces. I'm starting to wonder how I'll straighten this mess up. Once the word leaks out, it's practically impossible to erase the doubt that festers. And doubt is all these crazed cons need to ram a knife in a back.

I can't let Lorne deal with them alone. They've breached the codes and they'll have to taste joint justice for themselves. I think I can count on calling in a few veterans. I have my network—and these guys are dead serious. Many moons ago, we agreed to keep a loose affiliation and not hang around each other too often lest others recognize our bond. We decided to call on each other if ever the odds were to prove overwhelming. That's the best way to operate around here.

We'll confront these assholes and see how smug and smart they think they are then. They're cooked. They're going to get hurt, and hurt bad.

Paul, Franky and Benny are respected and feared

around here. Nobody, I mean nobody, messes with these guys. They respect everyone, keep a low profile and embrace the codes. I'm lucky and proud to have made a pact with them. But the need to call on each other has never come up until now.

I like to help the underdog and I've done things like this on my own countless times. I ensure the codes are adhered to. I've been doing this for years.

If anyone wants a piece of Lorne, I challenge them to come and get him, but not before they can prove what they're saying. Lorne isn't a rat. He's been set up by a bunch of low-life cowards.

Lorne says I shouldn't get involved, as I too am on short time, and in any case, he'll take care of these rotten bastards himself one day. One day! Today, man; it can't wait. What about a reputation? This will follow him wherever he goes. He can't hide from such things in prison. People can get him anywhere, anytime and when he least expects it . . .

Enemies on all sides, 1983

My buddy Bob is beaten up so viciously one day, I barely recognize him at lunch. His face is swollen and marked with black and blue bruises. Some muscle-bound kid pummeled him half to death for no apparent reason, except perhaps envy. I know Bob never bothers a soul.

Bob tells me the kid strode into his cell and started swinging without warning. The first blow felled Bob. He was almost knocked out on that first shot, but the kid kept swinging.

Infuriated, I storm out of the dining area and wait for the kid in the yard. Nobody beats up my friends for nothing.

The kid is walking around with a few of his buddies. He looks cocky. With a barrel chest and thick arms swinging at his sides, the kid struts like Rocky.

As I stroll over, our eyes meet. The punk has no fear and he looks like he's getting ready for a fight. No problem, punk. He says something to his friends, who look at me, then walk away.

The kid stands sideways and begins to loosen his neck muscles. His big head twists from side to side as he stretches his bulging pectorals under a tight-fitting white muscle shirt. He's a big kid weighing in at approximately 180. But is he a fighter or just a bodybuilder? I'll find out soon.

I'm calm. I'll see what happens once we get into it. I'm within a few feet of him now. My fists are clenched and my arms feel strong. My running shoes are tightly laced and my breathing is smooth. The air is fresh and cool and the sun helps keep my muscles loose. My shoulders relax and my stomach tightens a little.

The kid starts to tighten up. I can see veins in his

biceps stand out. I look at his chest, but I can see his hands and feet for any movement.

The kid remains motionless. I wish the punk would say something. I'm waiting for him to open up his fat trap before I slam him and break his jaw. But the kid is silent and won't move an inch. I can feel his friends looking at me, but they're not moving either. The situation is getting very tense. I'm getting anxious for the kid to say something or move.

The kid has been around for a while. He knows what this is all about. He knows there's no need for words. Maybe I have a good fight coming after all. I've never been beaten before and I don't feel like losing today. He'll have to work very hard and be very fast to beat me.

Anger surfaces and I feel the heat burn my face. Screw it, I'll initiate something. I feign a left jab. He moves backwards and shifts his weight, then moves back in with a right hand. The idiot is way too slow. Stepping into his move, I shoot a solid right hand of my own. The impact is vicious. The kid's head snaps back as my fist crashes into his contorted face. He's going down already.

His eyes roll in his head; he looks dazed. Twirling quickly, I slam him with a vicious left hook and watch his feet leave the ground. His head slams into the concrete wall as he falls heavily to the ground. He's unconscious.

Kneeling on his crumpled body, I slap him open-handed a few times to wake him up. He begins to snap out of the daze. Can the punk hear me? His eyes are straining to focus. I tell him I'll finish him off right here for keeps. He looks into the distance.

I slap him a few more times and he mumbles something. He can hear me. I ask him if it's over, or do I have to kill him right here and now because I don't care about anything right now. The kid doesn't say anything. I want to know if this is over, or do I finish him here? I mean it, and he better answer me right now.

He mumbles that it's over.

I go on to warn him to not come within ten feet of me or I'll take him out without warning. He nods.

Standing up, I watch him stumble to his feet. He's shaky and uses the wall to hold himself up. He walks toward the cellblocks but turns for the dining room. Dizzily, he turns one last time toward the infirmary. I know something is broken.

I see him five days later with wires in his jaw. He asks if he can come within ten feet and talk to me. I allow it. He apologizes and says he messed up . . .

Lorne looks surprised as he realizes for the first time the seriousness of his situation. The sun beating down on his sullen features, the kid shakes his

head in despair. He decides he'll get transferred to a
medium and get paroled from there . . .

Enemies on all sides, 1981

Sitting in my cell, I reflect on the lesson I've just
learned about crime and the administration of punishment. There's a lot more to it than meets the eye.
This day of discovery had revealed why these
lawyers, Crown attorneys and judges are so rich.
These charlatans are consummate conmen. I begin
to regard the cons with distrust and see them as
being naïve about the world they live in.

With my deal now fully sealed, I abandon my
escape plan. I figure I'll be paroled in approximately
two years. I have all my time calculated with mathe-
matical exactness. I figure I'll begin serving my sentence in a minimum-security facility and quickly
move to a camp, and from camp to a halfway house,
and right back out onto the street. I will avoid losing
as much good time as possible, but I do factor in
some additional time for occasional mishaps.

Another thought runs parallel to my calculations. I
feel deep guilt for what I've done. I feel I'm not being
punished sufficiently for the crime I've committed
and I want to suffer in prison. I want to serve hard
time and experience the pain and suffering the
system inflicts.

What if I walk out of prison in fifteen or twenty months? That's not a harsh enough punishment, is it? I don't think it is. I'm really confused. I must atone for the life I've taken, accident or not. Murder is murder and my victim is gone for keeps. The courts can call it manslaughter, but to me it's the same. I wish I could exchange my life for his, but . . .

I picture the funeral procession and my victim's weeping family. I hope they forgive me someday. I didn't mean to kill him. How could it have happened?

I'm called to see the classification officer and in less than two minutes he determines where I'll begin serving my sentence. He says I'm a candidate for Collins Bay, which is located near Kingston. I'm asked to sign my waiver of appeal and told to be prepared for transfer in less than thirty days.

Leaving his office, I'm shocked and dismayed at the news I'm not to begin at a minimum security because, as the officer said, I'm convicted of a serious offense and have a record of violent offenses against others. Property offenses are not viewed in the same light. I suspect the warden may have had something to do with my classification, the asshole.

I'm going to the penitentiary now, and that's completely new for me. Court is not new, except for the side I've just seen, but the pen is another dark world I know nothing about. What I thought I knew, I did not know at all, and what I do not know at all, I can only imagine.

If I said I'm not scared, I'd be lying to myself. The prospect of having to rub shoulders with some of Canada's most feared and notorious cons is terrifying. I know people are killed in those places for saying a wrong word. Dealing with the authorities and dealing with the cons are two different things. And if what I've just seen means anything at all, it means I'm a greenhorn at best. Even the most hardened criminals haven't experienced what I've just been through. The young lawyer even learned a few lessons in jurisprudence along with me.

To make matters worse, I receive some bad news from the street. Apparently some people are going to issue a contract to have me killed in prison for a drug ripoff they claim my brother pulled. The victims of the sting believe I'm the guy they want, and not my brother. It was a sizable ripoff, and some hitmen have been summoned from Toronto to take care of the matter. I imagine a good many cons will gladly take up the contract and try to kill me when I arrive. The threat is real and I feel very nervous about it.

Only a month before my incarceration, hitmen tried to kill my brother and me. We almost got caught up in a fusillade of bullets . . .

I'm called out of the range and told I'm being transferred. As two burly screws escort me from my range to the basement, the warden stops me on the main floor. Standing there in his ugly brown suit and thick black glasses, the warden says he wants to speak to me about something. Surrounded by his puppet soldiers, he sneers arrogantly. Hatred burns in his eyes and his mouth curls in disgust as he stares me down.

I react violently as a deep-seated resentment overwhelms me. The hatred consumes me with such force that I want nothing more than to slug him and rip his face off. I'm filled with fury and contempt. I let go a huge glob of phlegm in his face and tell him I'll come out alive, only to see him die. I mean every word I say and I plan to carry it out. The screws yank me away and rush me downstairs to the waiting bailiffs . . .

The gun-toting screw in his turret indicates the time for exercise is up. I'm pleased nobody has said a word or made a move against Lorne. I believe he is safe, but only as long as I remain in segregation. These guys will come back and kill him when I leave and I know it. Lorne better not go back to the yard when I leave. It's much safer to finish off his last four months in isolation and go home and stay out of jail. If he makes it to Joyceville or Collins Bay, the word will follow him there. The labels follow you across the country and remain—forever.

22

First Impressions
of the Haven

Millhaven, 1982

I'm shackled and cuffed as the sheriffs lead me cautiously into a long green bus fortified with barred
windows with green mirrors. Weaving carefully
through the "goose," as the guys call it, I glance at the
sullen faces. A dozen cons are seated on thin blue
seats, shackled at the ankles and securely cuffed.

My leg irons make walking difficult as I shuffle
along and then sit beside a monster who is solid
muscle and well over 200 pounds. I'm still infuriated
with the warden, and every muscle in my body is
tense. My face taut with tension and hatred, I look
blankly at my giant neighbor.

The big bear nods his humongous head and asks
me what's going on. He's very agitated too, and only
too eager to get involved. Without answering, I
shake my head, slide upright in my hard seat and
stare straight ahead.

We sit in silence waiting for the goose to lurch forward and take us to prisons across the province. Probably a few cases for Millbrook, Monteith, Maplehurst, Guelph, and maybe a few other pen-timers.

As I sit quietly, the scene with the warden is playing in my mind. The maniac thinks he's going to make me shake hard time. I know he's serious. He should have let the guys up on the range when I asked him politely. Now he's going to be dead meat when I get out.

The engine roars loudly as the bus begins moving away from the prison. Images dance through my mind when, driving through my home city, I catch glimpses of my old stomping grounds. We drive by the legal aid clinic where the police apprehended me eight months before. Images of my girlfriend, who had been stunned and shocked, haunt me. These memories hit me hard.

Picking up speed, the goose lurches by the President Hotel. A number of fight scenes flash in my mind's eye. The cops have whisked me out of that establishment at least four times. I remember the little mouthpiece who fell hard in the men's washroom that one night. I shattered his jaw with one good shot.

The bus brakes at the lights in the center of town, and I stare at the host of rounders standing around waiting to rip someone off or boost and sell enough goods on the black market to get drunk or stoned that evening. I don't recognize any of my old drinking buddies. The others don't have to worry about my crashing their party or smashing my fists into their drunken faces.

The fight scenes were brutal. Two guys in comas, one almost blinded, others sent by ambulance to the hospital, barely conscious—nothing more than human punching bags.

Rolling down the highway, my big neighbor begins to speak. He introduces himself as Ross and tells me he's from Sault St. Marie. I learn that he too is serving a five-year sentence and heading for Collins Bay as a first-timer in the federal system. Already we have a lot in common. Ross tells me he's done time in a few provincial jails. The big guy is very sociable and very talkative.

At some point in our conversation, Ross decides to share a few words about some younger-looking con seated at the back of the bus. Ross tells me the guy is a rat and he wants to go smash his nose into his face. Smiling, I encourage him to follow his instincts.

Ross lumbers to his feet and his curly black locks brush the top of the bus. He has shoulders like a football player. I'm certain the blue denim jacket clinging to his massive arms will tear at the seams if he starts swinging. As he makes his way casually to the back of the bus, the other cons observe him in awe.

Ross walks directly to his target, who is slouched on his seat, and, without warning, crashes his cuffed hands into the unsuspecting con's face.

The force of the blow causes the con's head to snap back violently. Bleeding, he brings his hands up and tries to protect himself. Ross swings his thick arms and lands a few more hard blows to the man's head and face. The victim's head rocks with the blows and the screws start to scream, but that doesn't deter Ross. Done with his vicious attack, Ross turns slowly around and returns to his seat.

The victim is moved to a caged enclosure farther to the back of the bus. The guy is still squirming and writhing and it's obvious his injuries are causing him serious pain. Ross mumbles a few words when he returns and nothing more is said about the assault.

Driving for hours on a dark and dreary January evening, we make a few stops along the way before the bus rolls into Kingston. This is the forbidden land of the penitentiaries . . .

A sullen hush has descended in the bus. The very first stop in Kingston is Millhaven super-maximum security—a notorious facility holding the most feared and dangerous cons in Canada.

Seeing this monstrosity for the first time, I feel anxiety in the pit of my stomach. The horror stories . . . its very name makes me nauseous.

Even Big Ross, in his bulging frame, is silenced by the presence of this infamous structure.

Lying silently amid brush and forest like some isolated fortress, the monstrosity is surrounded by two twenty-foot barbed wire fences. The place looks menacing . . . deserted . . . desolate . . .

Across the roadway, behind the bushes, some 200 to 300 yards away, we can see the blue azure of Lake Ontario. What a stark contrast. What a grim joke. Is the place escape-proof, I wonder? Just like Alcatraz was supposed to be?

My cousin Louis is somewhere deep within its bowels.

Looking out the side window of the goose, I contemplate a dull gray concrete tower that pierces the night sky. The turret looks like a miniature version of the CN Tower. Its circular top is a fortified, bullet-proof, dark-mirrored Plexiglas. The screw inside this thirty-foot turret is undoubtedly fully armed. He opens the first gate leading into the prison by pressing a button.

As we are driven past the first barrier, I stare at the prison's cold facade. Gray slabs of concrete are piled one on top of the other. There's not a soul to be seen.

Back in the bus, the sheriffs bark the name of the con who'll be staying at Millhaven. He makes his way from the back of the bus to the front. Sitting in silence, I begin to wonder how long it will be before I eventually darken the doors of this infamous hellhole. I know the warden back home is serious with his threats, and I know I'll be plagued by the administration wherever I go.

The thought strikes me that if I begin serving my time in a super-maximum prison like Millhaven, I couldn't be transferred anywhere else for screwing up, since Millhaven is the end of the line as far as lockup goes. I could be prison prey in Millhaven, and there's nowhere else to put me.

My attention is drawn back to the con making his way out of the bus. I can't shake the sight of his eyes. They're dark, and his face appears gray and deathly pale. His face is sullen, tight . . . expressionless. His heavy leg irons cut through the tense silence. The sounds of those chains cut right through me and chill me to the bone.

I decide at that very moment to stand up and make my way to the front of the bus. Without looking back at Ross, I walk toward the front of the bus and make my way outside.

When I meet up with the sheriffs, they panic and demand to know what the hell I'm doing outside. They try to put me back forcefully, but I resist. I'm telling them to save the government some money and leave me at Millhaven, because that's where I'm heading sooner or later. They're incredulous.

After a heated debate, I agree to get back on the bus. By this time, Big Ross has no idea what's going on and I won't tell him, either. This is my business and I'm not explaining to anyone the vindictive spirit of the warden back home.

I sit down on my hard seat with the sure knowledge I'll be in Millhaven before my five-year sentence expires. It's just a matter of time, and time is what I have on my hands. As far as I'm concerned, I've at least managed a peek at Millhaven before I come back here.

The thought of the con that's been dropped off keeps haunting me. Was his the look of a killer, I wonder? He seemed so distant and aloof to everyone and everything. It was something in his eyes and body language that told you not to bother him or you'd be killed . . .

Does it not stand to reason? People like screws have just the right profile to take on jobs like the warden's. You don't govern the beast, however. The beast has transformed you, as it did me and countless others. I've seen the madness and fury in your eyes. I've witnessed your twisted and demented ways.

The will to care deserts everybody after a while.

You can be aware of the wicked changes within yourself, but you can do nothing to arrest it. Soon you abdicate.

The warden's thick, black-rimmed glasses are smashed against his bloodied nose. He winces in pain as his eyes plead earnestly. Did you not carry out your personal vendetta against me, dog face? I had to contend with your cronies for seven long years, with 400 days in the hole, no parole and no privileges at all. Even my child had to be abandoned because I couldn't guarantee I'd be coming out alive.

I was sent into the valley of death among the callous, the psychos, the criminally insane . . . Your puppet soldiers had mastered the head games. They drove me crazy, and now I'll show you the results of your creation. I despise everything you stand for. You like to power-trip, don't you? A little dynamite under your car pales in comparison to seven long years of hellish torture, provocation and constant antagonism. I owe you . . .

23

The Jungle Range

The head of security is doing his rounds and I hear the guys calling him to their cell doors. I can imagine what these jerks are saying. The pompous ass loves it when the guys beg to be released from segregation. It gives him a sense of control and power. Strutting around with his fat screw, he assumes an air of confidence. The dumb ass has the job of assessing our cases and decides, along with the segregation review board, who'll be kept in segregation and who'll be released.

We're down here for a variety of reasons, and nobody ever knows when they'll be released. And that infamous clause in the Penitentiary Act that says "for the good order of the institution" is very broad and far-reaching. A guy can be kept down here for months. In any case, it really burns me up to see these so-called tough guys sucking up.

I call the sleazebucket over. He looks mildly surprised. The bald lizard figures he's broken my will. He thinks I'm institutionalized. Rubbing his hands together, he turns quickly and walks hurriedly to my cell. Yes, the repulsive reptile thinks he has me. His dark face bears a smirk.

Peering into my cell, he asks officiously what he can do for me. What can you do for me? Hmmm . . .

Rolling off my hard cot, shoulders hunched and head bowed, I paste a sad and remorseful look on my face. I ask him if . . . I begin to stammer and blush . . .

Composing myself, I look intently into his anxious eyes. He looks so happy, the idiot. I look down at my worn old running shoes, shuffle my feet, take a deep breath and let out a heavy sigh. I've got the idiot . . .

He asks me to say what I have to say.

Still with a sad face, I go on to ask if . . . well, if you could possibly

SUCK

MY

DICK?

Ha ha ha. I burst into hearty laughter.

His face reddening, he turns abruptly and walks angrily away. The entire range hoots and hollers. The pompous ass has encountered one con who doesn't care. What a blast; that was classic. I've been around these shithouses long enough to know they're nothing. I'll never suck up and I'll never ask these fools for anything . . .

The Bay, 1982

By the time the bus rolls to a stop at the entrance to
Collins Bay, the sheriffs have become my mortal
enemies. They'd witnessed Ross's assault on the
stool pigeon in the bus, and our personal encounter
at Millhaven draws the battle line. It's them and us:
the ones with the uniforms and bad attitudes, and
us with prison garb and our attitudes.

Sitting upright on the hard seats, I scan the tall
gray walls of the Bay. The walls are massive and
unending. They jut into the overcast horizon as my
mind conjures images of Russian circus acrobats
forming a human ladder high enough to get over. I
doubt they could.

I've heard that Collins Bay resembles Disneyland
and I'm not deceived on this point. Disneyland
doesn't have these oppressive walls, but this place
is probably a Mickey Mouse operation anyway. Lots
of games, I'm sure—head games.

My musing mixes strangely with the anxiety stirring in my gut.

In truth, the place is isolated and barren. But a few
yards away from this monster lives a whole community of thriving souls. These walls, however, contain
a community all of its own where people live out
their lives. What would a man do within these walls
for ten to twenty years? It's inconceivable.

The gates open wide and we're swallowed up

inside . . . I feel like I'm going to vomit. I'm at the mercy of my takers and there's no turning back. Gray, barren and desolate.

The gates of hell close up on me like a steel trap door and extinguish all hope . . . surrounded by thirty-foot walls, I'm being driven into a black hole . . . a dark abyss. My stomach heaves with anxiety and terror.

I'm labeled a rebel, and here I am pitted directly against the enemy in his corrupt domain. The bus slowly crawls deeper into this dark chasm of misery and torment.

Pulling my hands apart as far as I can, I feel the cold hard steel of my cuffs cut hard into my wrists. I don't want to feel the sensation inside my gut anymore. The stirring, it won't cease. My chest . . . it tightens and . . . and . . . and my body becomes rigid.

Clenching my teeth, I swear I can taste blood and chalk form in my mouth. My arms are as tight as steel bands, my stomach muscles constrict violently. I can't believe this hellhole.

We come to a stop. I look around the interior of the bus for the first time since leaving Millhaven and realize that Ross and I are not the only ones left on board. A handful of cons are being escorted off. Then my name is called out.

Petrified, I pull myself off my seat as my chains rattle underfoot. I must look like a real hardened criminal with my leg irons dragging on the ground. With my hands bound tightly at my waist with cuffs, the restraining belt renders me immobile.

Shuffling slowly, I make my way down the small steel steps and come to a steel door leading into the jail. Everyone is as quiet as lambs as we're admitted through the front gates.

My mind still reels in confusion as the screws line us up like cattle and methodically remove our chains. As I kneel on a hard wooden bench, my shackles are loosened. Another sheriff slips off the cuffs and restraining belt. They're pretty confident we're not going anywhere. And indeed we have nowhere to go.

As we are led deeper into the concrete jungle, door after steel door opens wide and closes behind us to emphasize their power and dominion over us. Every steel door deepens and confirms the depth of their grip on me.

Looking around anxiously . . . nothing but walls and cement surround me. The polished floors so common to institutions sound hollow underfoot. The echoes of my footsteps bounce off whitewashed walls and reverberate to my spine's center.

Tinted bulletproof partitions seem to speak to us as screws seek entry into more corridors and hall-ways. The labyrinth is so confusing I doubt I could retrace my steps if I were ever to take a hostage or disguise myself as one of these monsters. There are too many damned doors, and way too much confusion in my mind.

At last we come to two large steel-barred gates that lead to a long narrow corridor. It's so small . . . suffocating . . . the black soot of despair descends on me like a pall. The corridor is more than a hundred yards long. Peering down this narrow hallway, the persistent thought of how a man can live here forever hammers away at me. I just can't believe it. Sadness and sorrow envelop me. Despair and deep disappointment hit me hard. I feel hopeless and powerless. The place is so small.

I stand motionless. The screws begin issuing their hoarse commands. Someone behind the tinted partition responds and the gates of hell open up. I watch the electronic steel doors move apart as the mechanical engine hums quietly. That eerie sound sends tingles down the length of my spine.

Shuddering . . . everything is so deathly quiet . . .

Stepping cautiously into the corridor, I notice three cons lined up against the walls, gawking at us. What the hell is their problem? Hasn't anyone ever told them that staring is impolite? They seem so zombie-like.

This place . . . I won't ever understand the reality of this place . . .

As I head toward the end of the walkway, I catch sight of Big Claude. I can't believe it. My spirits rise for a moment when I see the big burly Frenchman. Claude and I had been partners in my hometown. We'd even tried to crack a safe together. He's walking casually down the hallway toward us and smashing his large fist against the wall. What a guy.

Big Claude, with his wide hairy chin and smiling dark eyes, immediately starts hurling insults and profanities in French. Stretching out his huge paw, he indicates in this thick accent that he's on his way to an appointment and that he'll come up to see me after. He says I'm on my way to the Jungle Range.

Perplexed by what he meant by the Jungle Range, I watch the big guy lumber away as my mind calls up a host of memories from back home. Big Claude is as strong as a bull and he doesn't take guff from anybody. He knocked out a policeman who tried to meddle in his fight in a tavern one night. He's a one-punch knockout kind of guy—and that suits me just fine.

We've fought side by side on a few occasions before and always won. We'll undoubtedly do so again if we have to. He's just as big as Big Ross, and just as crazy. I'll have to introduce the two big guys soon. I'm by no means a small lad myself, as I've put on another thirty pounds since my incarceration. At six feet and 180 pounds, I can fight as well as any of them. I figure the three of us will be well protected from any threat.

I'm still musing about seeing Claude and infused with a newborn confidence when we arrive at another steel gate leading to a long narrow range. This must be where the prisoners sleep. This must be the Jungle Range.

It's a two-tier setup. Thirty small cells are cramped together like stalls at the bottom and thirty more are set directly atop. The top row boasts a three-foot-wide catwalk edged by a three-foot-high steel railing.

The green, steel-barred cells face a bland wall with three barred windows at regular intervals. The range itself is no wider than thirty feet and holds a few plastic chairs and a square card table. A television is located at the far back corner.

Our section of the range faces east, while directly behind us another faces west, with our cells backing onto our neighbor's. Everything is designed to maximize living space. The two sections combined consist of 120 cells per range. A single steel-barred gate grants access to the two parts of the range, while another leads to the hallway.

The range is a bit longer than the entire width of

the cells combined. The cells being no wider than six feet, the range extends as deep as 190 feet. Thus, the total space of my living and sleeping quarters is about 200 by thirty feet. My personal cell is a mere seven feet long and six feet wide.

The escorting screws begin to spin the wheel that will unlock all of the cells simultaneously. The main wheel resembles a ship's steering wheel. Big Ross and I are going to be housed in adjacent cells. I'm to occupy B-17.

As the wheel unlocks all of the doors, we lift up a small steel latch and swing open our suffocating dungeons. This is home.

My new home for the next several months— perhaps years—consists of a small single bed set against a dull cement wall, with a steel toilet affixed at the back and a small porcelain sink set above. A small desk is crammed in across my bed and makes walking difficult. The cell is cold and sounds hollow inside.

To make everything worse, the television is blaring, as countless stereos are turned up to full volume. This is insane. I leave my cell and close my door as the screw spins the wheel and locks me out onto the range.

I look around. I see several cons seated at the back of the range watching television. The noise echoes throughout the entire length of the range.

Glancing at the upper tier, I hear some big black fellow yelling for the others to keep their music down. Nobody listens to anybody. I'm sure a fight will break out.

This can't be happening. How can anyone live like this? Big Claude told me I was going to the Jungle Range and now I understand what he means. Some of the most sordid drinking establishments I've frequented have more sense and order than this hellhole . . .

My door opens up. I'm to make a phone call to either an attorney or my family. The sheaf of legal-size paper with the dangerous offender application noted that I could have a representative at my hearing. Stepping out of my cell, I make my way to the end of the long narrow corridor. I pause momentarily to peek into Lorne's cell. Lying on his cot, he's all right for now. I nod and wink.

I'll call David Cole. He's very experienced with prison law and tactics. I've been jerked around long enough, and this is where it stops. I'm going to throw egg in their filthy faces. Eat crow. I'm going to get a good lawyer and we'll put it to you bastards this time. I've heard that you've tried this new Bill C-67 on a few cons already and failed. Davey boy had something to do with that. Yes, he'll help release me this time. You have provoked me and I've not taken it sitting down. Now you say I'm violent and likely to commit a serious offense when I'm released. Yes, I will, but what do you expect?

24

True Colors

I hang up the phone satisfied that David Cole will represent me. Looking at the fat screw, I smile. Should I go back to my cell peacefully? These door-knobs know how hard I can be to subdue, don't they?

My mandatory parole is not something to tamper with. It's MANDATORY. I'll show them I know how to beat the system. This place is crazy and violent, but I know a few tricks of my own. I've been taught very well, and by some of the best warriors. You guys won't win with me. You have no idea who you're dealing with. I can do my time. I have heart and soul and spirit, but you're cowards. David Cole will get me out of this one.

Back in my cell, I hear Big Pat playing his opera music. I like Big Pat. He always gives the screws a fight for their lives. What about that time he ripped his bed out of the floor and broke through a row of cell walls? That was great. What about that time when he slammed that big fat porker in the face with his cuffs on? He broke the pig's nose and knocked him out cold. Way to go, Pat. You don't take any guff from these jerks. You have to get out and take them out for keeps.

Good ol' Ury is down a few cells, and this giant of a specimen is extremely dangerous. He stabbed a guy in the gym area for God knows what reason. I remember when he first came to the Haven. He was timid and shy. What's happened to Ury? At six foot six and 230 pounds, he didn't need a knife. Did it feel good? Always wanted to know what it felt like to stick someone?

Little Wayne . . . can I call him Wiener also? He wants to give me his cassette of religious songs. How can he listen to this and kill people at the same time? How many years did he do in those special-handling units? Four, five years? This place is really something. Praying one minute and killing someone the next.

All the murderers are down here today. Some are being shipped out to the special-handling units; some are waiting for court dates for various murders they've committed in jail, while some just beat the living daylights out of a few other cons. One dropped some weights on a guy's head because he called him a goof. The guy's almost crippled and he'll be disfigured for life. This is good, because the victim will always think of the avenger when he looks in the mirror. I know the thinking.

Kenny, Derek and Moe are here because they beat up some of my hometown boys. Chris was kicked so hard in the groin he bled from his ears. He's in the infirmary now. Claude had to check in because Ernie was going to kill him, but I don't know for what. I guess it's none of my business, but I know they showed disrespect by changing the channel on the television set in the common room without asking permission.

I'm going to have to arbitrate this deadly dispute a little later, but for now I have to prepare for my hearing.

Just don't punk me off. I won't talk. I won't trust. I'll just let you have it . . .

The Bay, 1982

Before Big Claude gets back from his appointment, I encounter two more guys I know. I didn't know they were in this joint. I've spent many nights drinking, fighting, robbing and partying with Dave and Bo back home. In fact, Bo is one of the boys who'd done a lot of pen time and described the experience to me on a few occasions.

Bo was sent here two years ago. Ignoring my warning, he'd used one of my boosters for an armed

robbery. The kid ratted him out and now Bo's
locked up on a ten-year sentence.

A barrel-chested man with tattoos over every inch
of his large frame, Bo has a thick mane of reddish
blond hair and speaks from the corner of his mouth.

With a brief hello, Bo quickly pulls me aside. His
eyes anxious, he's excited about something. He
speaks quietly, then extracts a foot-long steel bar
from the back of his pants. He goes on to explain
there are two men on the other side of the range—
two men who have recently been transferred from
Millhaven—who want to see me. One of them is
named John.

Nervousness cramps my stomach . . .

My mind is still racing as Bo says he's not sure
what these guys want, but goes on to say they could
very well be hitmen hired to fulfill the contract on
me. Now I'm terrified. How could Bo even know
about the sting? How can this be?

Without another word, Bo hands me the bar,
turns his thick back on me and walks away with
Dave scurrying close behind.

I can't believe this. The pussies send me to the
lions' den and run away like yellow-bellied rats. I'm
tempted to use the steel bar on their empty heads.
Had I not helped these idiots on the street? Yes, I
had, and on more than one occasion. Then they just
abandon me, in the middle of the range, with a foot-

long bar stuck in the back of my prison garb. I
wonder what to do next. If I have any doubt about
my ability to survive, it's going to be put to the acid
test at this moment.

I begin to ask myself who these guys are and how
they know I'm here. These two cons are located on
the upper level in the middle of the range next
door. As far as I'm concerned, that's a good place to
be thrown from. I could be hemmed in on both
sides and ambushed on the way up. Somehow, they
know I've arrived and that worries me. How could
they find out so fast? Maybe they're henchmen for
the warden back home. If that's the case, they'll
suffer for their allegiance. Now I'm starting to get
pumped.

I feel the security and coldness of the steel bar
pressing against my back as I make my way to the
cells next door. Passing through the steel gate sepa-
rating the two sections of the range, I notice much
more movement and many more bodies on this side.

Glancing at the top of the landing, I perceive no
imminent danger, so I walk up the steps that lead to
the landing above. Arriving on the upper level, I
look down the length of the tier and see the cons
casually hanging around.

Keeping my eyes fixed, I make my way to the
middle of the tier. I visualize my fight plan in as
many positions as I can. If I have to, I could hurl the

guy over the railing without a moment's hesitation.

About halfway down the catwalk, I see a tall slender con standing near the cell I'm heading for. I try to determine if he has any hidden weapons, since he's not a physical threat. One punch could send him over the railing.

Keeping my eye on the slim con, I notice he's talking to someone in the cell. He looks back at me, expressionless . . .

He has those cold, dead eyes, like that guy who got off at Millhaven . . .

The con steps back a few feet and lets me look into the cell. I see a lone figure lying on a bed. I don't like his eyes, either.

I step back onto the tier, trying to stay aware of all movement around me. I ask the con in the cell if his name is John. He tells me he is indeed John and sits up and asks me politely to step into his cell.

Blue eyes and thin lips—this guy is way too smooth for me. Even his prison greens are crisp and his shirt immaculate.

If I went in, I'd risk having a knife driven through me before I'd be tossed over the railing. I may be paranoid, but I'm going to keep my distance.

Remaining at the entrance of his darkened cell, I ask John to explain what this visit is all about. He looks over at his friend, but both remain silent. I'm very nervous at this point, and waiting for someone to attack at any moment. I ask John once again to explain himself.

I listen hard for movement behind me. Realizing I'm not going to set foot inside his cell, John takes a crumpled piece of paper from his pants pocket.

Unfolding it a little, John says it's a letter from my cousin Louis in Millhaven.

I'm incredulous and more than a little suspicious. I've neither seen nor heard from my cousin in over ten years and I don't believe it's possible to get news from him this way.

John attempts to hand me the "kite," as a prison letter is called, but I decline, telling him he could read it to me instead. I don't want to put myself within striking distance at all. John looks perplexed. Unfolding the tiny scrap of paper, John begins to read in a low tone.

The letter is brief. My long-lost cousin Louis wants my help to distribute drugs inside the penitentiary. He'll furnish me with quantities of various drugs to be sold in Collins Bay.

John finishes reading the letter and fishes the equivalent of ten grams of hashish out of his upper pocket. Stretching out his arm, he attempts to pass me the package, but I don't take it.

Looking him in the eye, I tell him I've not seen my cousin in a very long time, but that's about to change. John looks confused and puts the hash back in his pocket. He presses me for an explanation. Shaking my head, I thank him and walk away . . .

The prison is filled with all kinds of potential dangers that few cons understand. To protect themselves they must consider their willingness to kill. But do they have the means? They may be able to punch and kick, but are they fast and hard enough? Can they shatter a jaw with one shot? Can they break ribs with a single kick? I wonder if they know how to get around a knife attack. What's their tolerance to pain? Can they remain conscious after a severe blow? Do they know how to roll with the force?

They have to be fast—very fast. I've seen takedowns, and it happens in fractions of seconds. A glimmer of a blade and then blood. Some of these guys have zip guns, and who says they won't shoot? . . .

The rope cuts deeply into his wrists as he twists his naked body against the rough tree bark. The still day brings a cool ocean breeze. Spreading the blueberries over his writhing frame, I wait anxiously for that black bear to come and satisfy his curiosity. His shiny black nose can detect these goodies for miles . . . a little meat to go along with your fruits. . . . Through the gray masking tape fixed firmly over this filthy mouth, the man tries to plead . . .

Bears like to keep to the same trails. This one will be rewarded for his habits. I hear the bear making his way through the thicket. He has a pig coming. Raw, but good nonetheless.

The bear approaches and begins to bite at the man's exposed genitals . . . I see tears and pain in his face . . . he is suffering—big-time.

25

My Ticket
to Millhaven

A legal-size manila envelope is slipped under my door. What the hell could it be this time? Hmmm . . .

Holy shit, it's the parole board again. My hearing will be in two days, and they've received notice David Cole will be representing me. This guy is fast.

My heart is racing and my stomach is jumping with excitement. Calm yourself, Ritchy, calm yourself. This is a miracle. Nothing short of divine intervention. I feel like I've just won the lottery. Wait, let me read this again . . . yep . . . that's it . . . the idiots didn't give me the six month's notice required to gate me.

Far out. This is a beauty of a technicality. This is surely cause for celebration. I'm going to be released for certain now. I can't believe it. Let 'er rip, Ritchy boy.

My time is up and the hour is near at hand. What a

rush. Screaming at the top of my lungs, I slam my feet against the solid steel door. My heart is pumping and my mind racing. Slamming on the door again, I yell in triumph . . . right on.

Let them squirm and twist over their failure. I'm coming out in a few days, and boy, do we have a date with fate.

Maybe this gating application was one big psychological ploy. Maybe they never intended to gate me, but rather to scare me with it. Maybe they want to keep that looming over my head, thinking it'll keep me out forever. But I'm not coming back here . . . never . . .

The Bay, 1982

Strolling out of the dining area after a greasy bacon and egg breakfast, Big Claude and I separate to perform our cleaning duties. We've agreed to meet each other at coffee break. I head over to 3 block and set to work. I sweep and mop the floor, clean the ashtrays, empty the garbage cans and set the chairs neatly in a semicircle.

Arriving back at the Jungle Range, I see four or five other cleaners and Big Claude sitting at a small card table sipping hot coffee. They motion to come and join them.

The talk centers on the prison and the cons. The

guys are discussing some tough and wild con who killed two shepherd dogs when the screws tried to subdue him. That story has me thinking and I wonder if I'll ever meet this madman.

I'm content, sipping my hot coffee and listening to the cons' war stories. The guys are talkative and seem very much at home. I wonder how long they've been inside this shithole, and for what?

Suddenly, the conversation stops. I follow the direction of their gazes and see a heavyset screw standing arrogantly at the end of the cellblock. His eyes are riveted on mine. Holding his stare for a few seconds, I look away and wonder if he's one of the warden's flunkies from back home. I start to get a real bad gut feeling.

The big goon barks an order to get up and finish my cleaning immediately. Embarrassed, I turn to look at Big Claude and the other cleaners. Some of them attempt to talk to the screw, but he ignores them. Now the guys look back at me and my embarrassment starts to turn to anger.

The screw is relentless. He barks another command to get up and finish my cleaning or I'll be placed on charge for disobeying a direct order.

I slowly get up from my chair and, looking into his menacing face, I burn fury into it. He glares back and tells me that I'll either listen to him or be put on charge for disobeying a direct order. At this point, I know what and who he is. There's no mistaking that fact.

Looking down the length of the range, I consider what I can do to salvage the situation. Tension is mounting and the guys are quiet. I know I can't let this screw center me out like this. What will the guys think? I'll be bothered by the cons if I don't do something.

The screw is now saying that I'll lose my job and be put back in my cell if I don't listen to him. He's pushing my buttons.

Feeling my anger rise, I'm more than ever convinced that this pompous ass is one of the warden's cronies and that my stay here at Collins Bay will be filled with such scenarios. There's no way I can tolerate this abuse.

The jerk then informs me that I've lost my job and I'll have to go back and stay locked up in my cell. I can't believe this scumbag.

Millions of thoughts run through my mind as, shaking my head, I walk to my cell and swing the door open. Sitting heavily on my cot, I contemplate my next move. The heat of anger's still burning my face as I hear the screw yelling down the length of the range, telling me to close my door so he can spin the wheel and lock me inside.

I can't take this shit and I won't be put down like this. What a first-class idiot. He doesn't know whose button he's pushing. There's only one way to deal with these rat bastards. Shotgun diplomacy it will be.

Sliding my hand into my steel cabinet, I retrieve the heavy steel bar Bo had handed me on my arrival.

Stuffing the bar in my pants down the small of my back, I emerge from my cell and look down the length of the cellblock and burn my eyes at the agitated screw. You want to play, let's play, bastard.

I walk down the hall to the screws' office. The screw who's pissed me off is there. As I peer through the glass, I see another screw is also inside.

Squaring off, I kick the thin wooden door. It flies open to reveal startled faces. Adrenaline pumping through my veins, I fly into the cramped office like a roaring volcano. I pull out the steel bar. The screw who taunted me stays behind his desk.

Picking up the tempo, my mind racing, I'm pumped and I'm pissed. Screaming at the top of my lungs, I rave like a lunatic who's completely out of control. My eyes are bugged out, my body as rigid as a board, I'm sure I look insane.

They're frozen with fright. Too late, you sniveling scumbags. Steel bar firmly in hand, I bring it down inches from their faces and smash it onto the desk. The ear-shattering crash reverberates inside the small office.

One screw tries to focus his mind on a book he's just picked up and placed on his lap. I kick the book out of his hand and it flies through the air. Swinging the bar inches from his head, I crash it against the glass panels inside the office. Shards of glass explode in all directions. The screws start to shake. The jelly-kneed jerks are horrified now.

Mocking the screws, I ask them to repeat the charges. They've become deathly quiet. The assholes have nothing to say now. I can see they're terrified and wish they had never said a word to me. The fools are motionless. Quiet as mice. Completely caught. Helpless.

They have become my prisoners.

Glaring menacingly at the screw who's had me charged, I tell him to kneel down and give his friend oral sex. When he hesitates, I swing the bar inches from his head and smash another pane of glass. The screws look at each other with humiliation and fear.

That's what you get when you push me. Get up and show me what you can do. I'll kill you today. I've nothing to live for anymore. I've lost it all. I want to die and I'll take both of you with me . . .

They're petrified and begin begging me. The rat bastards are paralyzed with terror. I tell them to call Millhaven and have a car pick me up in an hour while I wait in the office with them. Meanwhile, we'll have a good time.

As the screw reaches for the phone, I crash my steel bar inches from his trembling hand. He recoils and stumbles backward over his seat onto the floor. I feel like driving my fists into their putrid faces . . . to slam their ugly mouths . . .

I'm jumping in my cell with glee and unsurpassed excitement. My mind is reeling and my heart swelling. Have to party, man. Have to release this energy surging through my body. Incredible. Today is Prisoner's Justice Day and justice has prevailed. Moreover, the screws don't want to give us tea during jug-up—just another deliberate attempt to cause problems. Okay, dickheads, I think this is a great opportunity.

It looks good on some of the guys, but unfortunately I too have to pay the price for stupidity. Why did some of these cons observe the screw's day of silence for comrades who'd been killed in Archambault Penitentiary?

I met Willy and Jay in Kent maximum security and saw what the screws did to them after that murderous riot. These guys were tortured and brutalized. They stuck a billy club up a guy's ass. Can't the guys see the line of cleavage, or do I have to draw them a picture? How could the guys even begin to contemplate letting the screws commemorate their dead? To even participate in their day of mourning! First-class idiocy, I say. First-class.

The screws deserve to die. They're brutal and barbaric. They drive the guys to murder. Why else would the guys kill them? For nothing? For fun? The fact remains that it's them and us and no amount of joint mourning can ever bridge that chasm. Our history is long and vivid. How many men do you think they killed?

To hell with it. I can incite something here. What should I do? The guys look pretty pissed and pumped already. I can feel the tension in the air. It's just ripe for some action. The parole board may as well get a good fresh look at me. Yes, it's the perfect opportunity to go out with a big bang.

26

Inside Millhaven

I have to devise disruption. Prisoner's Justice Day, August 10, is a time to commemorate our dead. Men have been shot on the fences in a mad scramble to escape this senseless and brutal regime. Men have starved themselves to draw attention to our plight.

Today, we have televisions and radios. We have clean clothes and a shower every day if we're in population. We have trailer visits and receive paroles. We have many amenities that were not available to generations past. They've shed their blood for us. They're martyrs.

How many men have committed suicide in here? How many have been falsely imprisoned? How many have been murdered? We don't have to break rocks, as prisoners did in the past. We don't have to carry wheelbarrows full of gravel from one place to the next. We don't even have to work in here if we don't want to.

The screws don't respect our efforts and our

plight. They couldn't last a day in these holes. They couldn't tolerate the isolation and the barbaric mentality we're confronted with daily. They don't care if we live or die in here. Every day is a challenge to stay alive. God knows when someone will stab us in the back or come up and slit our throat. Sure, we messed up and landed in here, but where is just and fair punishment? These idiots go overboard and get personal.

We're the ones who have to live in the trenches. We're the ones who've lost our freedom and forsaken our family and friends. We all have a conscience. We have feelings too. Being locked up like an animal for ten to twenty years would make anyone crazy. It's kill or be killed around here, and nobody can change that mentality.

We have no rights. We're the civil dead. We can't take our grievances to court. We're subject to beatings, gassings and long periods of solitary confinement on grounds of simple suspicion. What kind of justice is that?

As long as they get their twenty-five dollars an hour to torture and antagonize us daily, they're happy to be feeding their families. We owe our pioneers a debt of gratitude. We can remember them with one day of fasting.

These men have died within this very monstrosity, probably in the cell we currently occupy. The walls speak of their pain and suffering. Their blood stains the walls and their screams of terror emanate from the cold slabs of concrete surrounding you. Feel the pulsating rage beating from your own concrete slabs. Listen to the heart-wrenching pain echoing down from generations past. Can you not see the pain and loneliness within your own souls? It pales in comparison to years not too far in the past.

Jack self-immolated while he was in solitary confinement for two years. Brian's testicles were stapled to the table during a police interrogation. Larry had a billy club pushed up his ass. Moe had a gun pushed through his front teeth. Mike had his head cracked open. Louis was tossed down a flight of stairs, cuffed to a chair. Just the other day, Bobby was mobbed and slammed like a rag doll by the goon squad.

We ourselves have killed men. Life has no value here. This godforsaken place has turned us all against one another. It has turned us into . . . into . . . into what exactly?

How dare they not acknowledge our dead? It's their hand that's killed them. I know how to create havoc and deathly risk. I'll disrupt the count. I'll have everyone block their windows with paper and brace themselves against their walls so the screws can't open the cell doors. Even if they open the food ports, they won't be able to see us.

We'll force them to open our doors. They'll have to bring the goon squad, billy clubs, tear gas and mace guns, shields and armor . . . let's get it on. This is one Prisoner's Justice Day they'll never forget. They want a fight, let's give them a fight. All right then, another ultimatum. They'll respect and honor our dead or risk being killed.

Ury the giant has his window covered and his door braced. Ury is big at 230 pounds. Big Pat is also in line, and he goes to 250—nothing short of a Sherman tank. There are at least ten guys in here that weigh over 220 pounds of solid hatred and muscle. These will give the screws a fair run for their money.

There's no easy way for the screws to get the count done now. They'll have to pry the doors open one at a time. There are thirty doors in this segregation unit, and they hold the most dangerous cons in Canada.

We'll flood this shithouse and let the riot rip through the night, the next day and many nights after that. We'll cause millions of dollars in damage to this infested monstrosity.

I hear the screws coming into the range and they're asking the con in cell 1 to show himself. The kid is silent and disobeys a direct order. Way to go, fella. I peer through my cell window and see the battery in their full riot gear. Billy clubs, mace guns and tear gas in hand, they look exasperated and worried. Dickheads. What are they going to do when they have to open my door? I have a surprise for you in here.

Ury is smashing his huge feet on his door and the sounds are terrifying. I wouldn't want to be the one to calm him down. No way, amigo. Big Pat has already knocked out a few of you screws and he's getting pumped up big-time right now. The mace is like perfume to Big Pat. This is great.

The screws are threatening to toss tear gas in cell 1. Let them blast away. It'll burn, but it won't kill. Make sure you spit and throw shit at them before they take you down. We'll mess up the count again on the next hour. We'll burn these militants right out. They'll plead for the end, but we'll never relent.

The kid is strong and he has heart. He's not afraid of their stupid tear gas. After a great deal of effort the screws manage to open his door and rush in. I hear cursing and a vigorous wrestling match going on. I can't see, but I can hear that the kid is putting up a valiant effort. It's taking quite a bit of time in there. He must be putting up quite a fight. The kid is swearing and threatening and the guys are getting worked up even more. Good.

The screws emerge from cell 1 drenched and heaving. One asshole is cursing under his breath as he looks in the direction of my cell. They have over-heard my organizing and they're getting fed up with me. Eat crow. Come on and see what you can do.

The screws are heading for Ury's cell. How are they going to deal with this giant? Here they come, Ury. Give it to them, big guy. You only have a few years left and you have a definite release date. They can't alter your sentence that much.

The monsters have opened his food port and are going to spray him with mace. I hope he has the presence of mind to keep his clothes on. Ury will terrorize these goons.

What am I hearing down there? What the hell is it with Ury? He's not giving them much of a battle. This is very disappointing. I thought he'd at least give them a fight for a few minutes. This guy is incredibly strong. I've wrestled with him in the gym and felt his strength. What the hell is it with Ury?

I'm disillusioned by these so-called tough guys. All he had to do was wrestle them and force them to physically take him to the hole. He's not putting up any fight at all. The kid in cell 1 did a much better job, and he's only five foot nothing to start with. I'm losing respect for this guy. He's afraid to pick up more time? What the hell is it? They're taking Ury to the hole and he's chained in less than two minutes. It won't be that easy with me . . .

Millhaven, 1982

The Collins Bay authorities have no reservations concerning my unorthodox request for a transfer to a higher-security institution, although they'd prefer to keep me in solitary as long as they can. Aware of their desire, I prepare my strategy carefully. I will seek to be transferred as soon as possible.

The screws are reluctant to come near my cell in solitary because they risk having piss tossed all over them. I figure if I raise enough fuss with the front-line workers, the heads of the institution will expedite my transfer. I set fires in my cell, as well as electrical traps. I steal a butter knife and begin sharpening it to a lethal point.

I'm forcibly taken to institutional court and handed more than fifty days in solitary. Leaving the kangaroo court, I tell the judge I'll break the screws' spirit before I complete this sentence. It becomes a battle to break my will.

They try to increase the intensity of their punishment by placing me in the Chinese cell—an empty room with a hole in the floor for a toilet—but that has little effect on me. I merely scream and curse and escalate my threats. I tell them they'll have to open the door sooner or later and a price will be levied on the first screw in striking distance. This thought sobers them up a bit and they begin to plead with me to relax; they have no quarrel with me.

After less than five days in solitary, the sheriffs arrive to transfer me to Millhaven. My strategy has succeeded. The screws have pleaded with the heads of the institution to get me transferred. I'm a bad influence to the good order of the institution, they say.

When the sheriffs arrive, I muse that they should have listened to my request when we first arrived at the gates of Millhaven ten days before. The government could have saved the expense of coming to pick me up . . .

The ride from Collins Bay to Millhaven is emotionally rough as I gaze out the car window at the beauty of nature and free people milling about. Here I am, shackled and cuffed like some rabid animal while folks carry on their usual business. It's a beautiful sunny day as I sit in the back of the sheriff's car looking at the trees and the view of Lake Ontario that stretches before my eyes, juxtaposing freedom and confinement. I remain silent for the entire ride and breathe in the beauty and freedom I yearn for.

A moment of lucidity surfaces. I must somehow quell the incessant longing for freedom. I have over forty long months to serve before I ever see the streets again.

The car approaches Millhaven . . .

With its turrets and the barbed wire electronic fences surrounding it, Millhaven sits in isolation. Born of violence, its reputation is notorious.

These physical structures and their inner workings reflect man's basest self. Who could believe these institutions could rehabilitate the cons? Anyone who darkens the doors of the infamous institutions becomes a hapless victim of this mad realm. People are forced to adopt a mentality that guarantees them neither peace of mind nor one sliver of security. They become subjects of a surrealistic existence where violence and mayhem rule supreme.

I'll soon darken the doors of that mysterious and notorious beast and experience its wrath and pulsating rage. Not too many hometown boys who've ever been in Millhaven have discussed their experience there.

I'm at the gateway of hell and about to discover what lies behind the menacing and monstrous face of Millhaven.

I'm sitting quietly in the back seat of the green corrections car as the first steel barrier opens with the low hum of an electric motor, as the grating of steel cuts to my spine's center. My stomach taut, I begin to question the wisdom of my decision to be transferred.

The screw in the control tower opens his tinted bulletproof window and looks contemptuously down on the car as we pull in between the twin twenty-foot barbed-wire fences. The first fence closes behind us before the second opens up. This damned pit is swallowing me whole . . .

The second fence slides open and the car rolls forward a few yards and then stops abruptly. The sheriffs hop out and lead me, chained and shackled, to a small outpost where a thin screw with a long crooked boxer's nose takes the information from my escorts.

Everything is so quiet . . . subdued . . .

The sheriffs motion me through a steel metal detector inside the small office before we proceed toward the front lobby of Millhaven. Taking a hard long look at the front of the building, I know it will be many months before I ever see this side of the beast again.

Will I ever see it again? That thought makes me shudder . . . I'm feeling disconnected and out of sorts . . . dissociated. . . .

Inside the prison, I'm led through a labyrinth of corridors and countless doors. The beast is built in this fashion to purposely confuse the newcomer . . . it's a maze . . .

Something deep inside me stirs . . . mixes anxiously the deeper I'm led inside. I can feel an undercurrent of something I can't readily identify. What is it with this putrid place that it sends these foreboding feelings running through me? I just can't put my finger on it . . .

Pushed deeper into this tomb, I note that the familiar smell of antiseptics common to hospitals permeates the institution and the polished floors and barren walls are strikingly similar too. I'm beginning to think I'm walking into a mental institution for the violent criminally insane.

This place is nothing like Collins Bay. There's something fundamentally different here. But what the hell is it?

Suddenly, I begin to understand why my innards are twisting like serpents. It has to be the deadly tension. I've heard other cons mention this tension. They said you could cut it with a knife. . . . It's suffocating and it sinks into my soul while it throws a veil over my eyes.

The tension must be the product of the deadly earnestness and utter cruelty of both the screws and the convicts. It fills the stale air and pastes itself on their faces like a mask of fear.

Numbed and disoriented, I'm handed over to the institutional screws like excess baggage thrown out of the sheriffs' garbage site. They turn their backs to leave, but not before saying a few words about what they'd learned about me from Collins Bay.

My reputation had started in Sudbury and haunted me in Collins Bay. Now that I'm in Millhaven, I can't very well be viewed as a model inmate. I'll survive one way or another . . . I hope.

The stern-looking screws at Millhaven are leading me through many more corridors . . . my stomach cramping with every step . . . where the hell is everyone? The thought crosses my mind that everyone is locked up. There's no movement here.

As we enter a dome, I understand. This is the center and heart of the prison, where its rage is pumped out to its tentacles . . .

The dome is huge, its ceiling towering . . .

The doors are not barred; they're wrought iron, like on fancy verandas. Something has reached deep inside me . . . is stirring . . . modern torture . . . I can feel it already . . .

Proceeding through the dome, we pass countless gates and arrive at a range of cells. The steel barrier is opened electrically and I'm led to a cell.

Everything in this monstrosity operates by electrical power. Nothing is done manually. All control is channeled through control towers equipped with countless little buttons. These tinted bulletproof glass enclosures are the brains of the prison. But who's inside that dark bulletproof glass? I see a dark silhouette, but does he have a gun? How does he get in and out of that cubicle? I can't see any doors . . . he must come through underground tunnels.

Arriving at a cell, I see the door is a light blue steel slab that is two inches thick. My window facing the range is a three- by six-inch opening covered with two-inch-thick bulletproof glass.

As I walk into my cubicle, the door slides shut with a reverberating echo . . .

Barren, desolate, cold . . .

My toilet is made of shiny aluminum and a sink is fixed directly above it. The one-piece prefab is dull silver and cold to the touch. The spring bed is small and covered with a striped mattress two inches thick. At the head of my bed is a window looking out into the prison yard and, beyond the fences, into the woods. The window is fortified with steel bars three inches in diameter and is covered with plastic slats. A plastic knob jutting from the wall allows me to raise and drop the slats.

The corner of my cell is equipped with a small metal desk and a bright orange plastic chair. The color is out of place.

A dull gray metal screen hides my radio. Probably some form of listening device as well.

I might as well be standing in the six-foot metal locker that will serve as my closet. It's a foot and a half wide, empty and gray.

There are thirty such cells on this range. A nine-foot corridor separates fifteen per side. I can't see into the cell across the narrow corridor because the cells are slightly staggered.

Everything is very quiet. Silence is supreme compared to the Jungle Range at Collins Bay. But this is way too quiet . . .

Ury looks defeated with chains around his thin black ankles . . . they glitter . . . the leather restraining belt gives his V-shaped torso the look of an Olympian. I've seen him effortlessly perform deep squats with 400 pounds on the bar. Preacher curls were performed repeatedly with 160 pounds. The guy can move like a cougar.

27

Learning the Ropes

Too damn quiet. No heart. And no soul. Solidarity among cons is a myth. The chicken shits won't smash and burn this place to the ground because they're afraid to lose their privileges: visits, transfers, parole. They're worried about not getting their dope supply. As far as I'm concerned, they're a bunch of assholes. I hope I see their cowardly faces on the street. They'll undoubtedly be drunk or numbed out on heroine when I smash 'em.

These so-called tough guys like to play the big shooters in here, but I know they're just a bunch of yellow-bellied scum who prey on old ladies when they're out on the street. The jerks can make this place their home, but I'll never be made a robot by any institution.

Except for the stool pigeons in this shithouse, these big shots would be hurting big-time. I'll see to it that nobody gets paroled at my expense. I'll see them on the street and dummy them up once and for all. I wish I could bomb this damned shithouse. I wouldn't lose an hour's sleep after the big bang.

I've broken jaws, cracked ribs and flattened a few noses here. Punking me off with their tough-guy attitudes, they end up bleeding and mangled. The sound and the feel of bones crushing against my knuckles is so good. Almost as good as the sight of their battered bodies hurtling through the air. I don't need a shank or a pipe. I can kill them with my bare hands. If I could, I'd lash out at every opportunity, but I don't want to risk staying here forever . . .

Millhaven, 1982

I hadn't seen or heard from my cousin Louis in over ten years—with the exception of his kite in Collins Bay—when he appears at my cell in Millhaven. He has cartons of cigarettes with him, which I decline because I want to remain physically fit in this strange and dangerous place. Louis also offers to have me transferred to his section in population so he can teach me the ropes. To this I agree. When I'm transferred to his range, we set up an appointment for my indoctrination . . .

Waiting in my cell, I begin to think about Louis. He's five-ten, 160 pounds and stalks like a tiger. His short dirty-blond hair is cut neatly, his clear blue eyes shift nervously over a long thin nose and his thin lips are taut. I remember hearing about my cousin Louis as a kid. He's the black sheep of the family, they'd say.

I recall the time his parents discovered dynamite under their porch. They were afraid Louis was going to blow up the house. The family feared and avoided the kid. He was bad news.

He'd disappear for years.

On one of his long-awaited returns, Louis hid a suitcase full of guns, disguises and cash at my sister's house. That was a shocker. He'd robbed a bank and made a hasty escape. While the police were investigating, Louis was robbing another bank a few blocks away . . .

He arrives at my cell at the appointed time eager to begin my lesson. Sitting quietly on my bunk, I watch Louis light a cigarette and slowly let out the smoke. Sizing me up, he commences to speak in a way that surprises me. Louis is very articulate, pausing and thinking before he speaks. He weighs his words carefully.

I certainly didn't expect my cousin to be this smart as a self-taught con . . .

"Millhaven is a super-max where Canada's most ruthless live and die. You'll find all kinds and breeds of deviants here, ranging from cold killers to the basest of child molesters, stool pigeons and rape hounds. It's open season on these undesirables, but they remain well buried in the ranks.

"It would be better if you did your own time and didn't bother the less-favored elements. There'll be enough trouble knocking at your door without having to go looking for it.

"Psychos are everywhere. Personality conflicts are resolved at the end of a knife or a pipe. Be on your toes and don't underestimate anyone. The mentality here is unlike anything you've ever seen or heard. Don't trust anybody.

"It's time to drop 'friend' from your vocabulary and replace it with 'acquaintance.' You don't make any friends in the Haven.

"You could be killed or seriously injured in here. Stabbings and violent assaults are common and happen quickly. It doesn't take very much effort to walk by someone and drive a shank into his back.

"Many takedowns occur during changeovers. This is when all the prison doors open for four minutes every hour on the hour and cons move from one place to another. Traffic is heavy during this period, and the predators know how to conceal themselves. They find their blind spots and wait for their target. There are many blind spots around the prison; I'll show you some of them later.

"It's important for you to change your routine from time to time. The predators know how to stalk their prey. Change the times of your workouts and other regular tasks if you suspect trouble. Without exception, if you feel and think about getting violent with someone, you can be sure they're thinking the same.

"When trouble does come, try to resolve the matter without violence, if possible. Go prepared and take the initiative, and don't allow conflict to fester. It'll turn on you.

"If you can't settle it that way and feel like you're backed in a corner, then come out like a tiger. It may warrant playing for keeps.

"View this place as a valley inhabited by the most calculating and sinister killers. That being so, see yourself as the most calculating, callous and cruelest of them all.

"Show respect for everyone and be prepared to come out of your corner if you're ever pushed into one. Strike as fast as lightning and as hard as a mule. Take 'em down and make sure they stay down. Make sure they won't come back to finish you off later.

"You may have to take it to the limit. If you're using a shank to take someone out, spread shit on the blade. This way, if they don't die from blood loss, they'll die from infection.

"It goes to the limit around here, cuz. It means playing for keeps. As such, it's a good idea to wake up in the morning, look at yourself in the mirror and tell yourself today is a good day as any to die . . ."

Pausing, Louis draws a long drag on his cigarette as his eyes look deep into mine. Although I'm scared by everything my cousin has just told me, I try to keep myself calm. My worse nightmare could not have revealed what he's just described.

Letting out another long stream of smoke, Louis rubs a hand over his jutting chin. Biting his lower lip in concentration, he resumes . . .

"If queers or queens make approaches, politely refuse. If they make a second pass, take 'em out.

"Drugs and alcohol are everywhere and I urge you to avoid that trip. Ninety percent of all killings revolve around the dope scene. I know of men who've been carved open because of dope. One con had his ass split open to get at his dope stash.

"Don't accept anything from anyone, because you don't want to put yourself in a position where you'll have to repay the favor. Nothing is free. Cons can manipulate in many ways.

"It's in your best interest to avoid cliques. You'll be spending a lot of time on your own—it's much safer that way. Don't encourage conversation with anyone. Be brief and polite. Nod your head or say a quick hello and move along.

"Don't promise anyone anything. Don't look into

anyone else's cell—that's their only privacy. It's sacred.

"Adopt the three-monkeys attitude of not seeing, not hearing, not talking. Don't ask questions and do your own time. Remember that we go to the limit in here.

"Stay quiet and mind your own business. You'll step over fallen bodies, but ignore them. There's a sordid tale behind every casualty.

"By all means, remain fit and be prepared to fight like a tiger if you're ever pushed into a corner. But never reveal your abilities. You don't want anyone to know what you'll do when trouble comes. The unknown is what scares people and it's your best weapon. Also, if these guys know you'll take it to the limit, you'll never survive the attack. It's kill or be killed.

"Let me tell you about the screws. They're the enemy. They've been known to issue contracts on us. We have retaliated. I know in my own case a screw was placed under surveillance for a few days and given a friendly warning. The guy received a detailed letter outlining his activities, including the time and place of his bowel movements. That shook him up and he subsequently left us alone.

"We don't talk to the man. If we do, it's because we need their services as pack mules. They pack

what we can't possibly obtain through regular channels. The cons stuff bundles of dope and cash up
their ass. Coke, heroine, you name it, we can get it.
That's the regular route. But greater amounts
involve the screws. Pounds of coke, grass and hash
pass through our hands.

"The screws will try to get under your skin, but
ignore them. They'd like to make you shake rough
time, if they can. Misery loves company and they're
miserable bastards. They know you'll respond when
they press the buttons, but ignore them.

"The administration also uses the carrot system.
They dangle trailer and regular visits, transfers to
lower-security prisons and even paroles in front of
your face in return for information and conformity
to their rules.

"The best way to handle that is to forget about life
on the street and regard this place as home for the
next few years. This will not only eliminate the
carrot system, it will also help you shake better
time. Just remember you're at the end of the line, so
you're not in a place you'll get early parole.

"After all, you're only serving five years. Most
lifers here are serving ten to thirty. So don't play the
game. I also suggest you not tell anyone you're a
short-timer because that's a weakness. The cons
may think you would never risk prolonging your
stay by defending yourself to the limit."

Louis's voice trails off as the doors open, signaling changeover. My mind on the lesson, I know this is a time to be careful. I look Louis in the eye and assure him I both understand and appreciate his words and experience.

Looking back at me, he says I've acquired the basics to survive . . .

Screws burst through in a frenzy. Their hands and bodies are everywhere. One of them pulls at my arm and I twist his wrist easily. He grimaces and yelps. Hands grope at my hair and arms wrap around my neck. I throw myself into the air, slam my feet on the concrete wall, and we fall on my hard cot. The slime-ball beneath me gets an elbow in the guts. He exhales loudly. Good.

Turning on my stomach, I get up with two goons hanging on me like bloodsuckers. I feel good. I love this shit. They can't hold me. Backing away, they point their mace gun at my face. I throw out my hand and grab hold of the gun. They register shock that I have the damn thing in my hand. Right on. Let's see if *they* like this orange juice. I squeeze the trigger, but it's on safety. They lunge forward and we wrestle some more. They push me onto my cot and hold my legs. I feel like kicking, but I know I'll be put on charge for assault. They can't charge me if I only resist, though.

They bring out the cuffs, seize my left arm and try twisting it. They can't move it. I bring my arm closer to my chest and turn swiftly. Now the mace gun is trained on my face. Let him shoot, because his friends will get some too. He won't do it.

28

Time in the Big House

It took them a while to get me back to the hole and I hope the guys in seg will rock the foundations of this shithouse for a few days. To maintain our basic human rights and exercise our power of choice, the spirit to fight has to be practised daily. Nobody ought to accept oppression, provocation and unjust bullshit without a fight. The sword is mightier than the pen in here. Shotgun diplomacy all the way. We must hit them where it hurts—money—through damages and work stoppages.

I know I have to send a message. Have to deliver it forcefully but without raising suspicion. Preparations will be made and the plan carefully executed. Nobody has ever serial-killed those involved in the administration of criminal justice ... not until I'm released onto the streets.

I know their names and know they live here in

Kingston and surrounding areas. I'll stalk, track and capture them. There are so many things I can do with freedom, violence, patience and intelligence on my side.

I know the streets in Kingston are well protected and under surveillance. I know that the police monitor strangers and that such communities implement community watch groups. The screws have ways to keep a close eye on one another if one of them goes missing. I'd be paranoid too if I spent most of my waking hours hurting people. They prey on the defenseless and carry on with impunity. They delight in provoking and hurting us.

The screws show up at my door and say my parole hearing will occur in two hours. They want to know where I'm going when I'm released. I tell them I'm going into hiding and they won't find me until I come knocking on their doors or sneak through their windows late at night. I advise them I'll catch them coming out of the tavern or slip through their back car window and wait for them as they come out of the mall.

Concerned, they look at one another and demand that I tell them where I'll be going. I don't have to tell them dick all.

Angry and threatening now, they say I won't be paroled unless I give them a specific destination. Kingston, I tell them. The woods in Kingston. I'll become a squatter in your hunting and recreational grounds. We'll see each other on the hiking trails and have a nice talk. You won't recognize me, though.

Desperate and exasperated, they say I'm issuing threats. But I know the time for threats is no more. I'm being released and there's nothing anybody can do to arrest that dreadful reality. Unless of course you're prepared to kill me right here and now . . . come on in and try it, I say . . . come on in.

The idiots walk away with fear written all over their ugly faces. They've gone too far for far too long. Countless days in the hole, fabricated charges, wrongful convictions in the kangaroo courts, incessant provocation, constant antagonism, human violations, unparalleled, regular and unceasing head games and absolute bullshit all the time. I'm not prepared to let all this misery go unpunished . . .

I'll never forget these putrid, rat-infested infernos. Puppet soldiers perpetuating acts of brutality, mayhem, torture and misery . . . how I wish I could hug my big old tree. Squirm, you mothers, because the party is just beginning. Come on, you fat swine, come on out and let's take a joy ride . . .

The fat old judge staggers to his bare feet as he wipes the dirt off his wrinkled forehead. Pain and terror pasted on his face, he looks up out of the pit with resignation. You're going to take a ride you'll never forget, Your Honor . . .

I pull him out and lead him to my old pickup. Cuffs have already been secured to the hitch on the back bumper. The metal glitters in the sun as the engine rumbles quietly.

The bastard begins to snivel and grovel as I secure his feminine hands with the cold hard steel cuffs. Naked, he shivers as the thin gray hair on his back blows lightly in the cool wind blowing off the ocean.

Jumping into the driver's seat of my old truck, I step down on the accelerator and hear the engine roar fiercely. The bastard is going for a ride.

Gravel flies as the truck lurches forward and the judge's carcass brushes against the hard gravel road.

Slamming the brakes, heart beating madly, I dash to the rear of my murderous vehicle.

GAADD . . . I can't believe it's the same stupid asshole . . . pink flesh dangling, blood oozing everywhere . . . a trail of human entrails.

The judge is still breathing . . . the will to kill is surpassed only by the will to survive . . . too bad. Back in the pit you go, dogface . . .

Millhaven, 1982

Millhaven is a barbaric dungeon. Tough, huge and ugly cons roam the corridors of this monstrosity, looking to spill blood. Steel bars and pointed swords become extensions of their tree-trunk arms.

Dead eyes stare straight into nothingness, the mind is devoid of compassion. Bodies pile up in the gym and two-by-fours slam onto craniums as the cons make a hasty retreat into dark corners.

Intimidation and cruel savagery are how they exert control. The tension is so thick you could cut it with a knife. The deadly aura hangs over everything like a dark cloud; it's kill or be killed.

The anxiety produced by deadly confrontations leaves you numb with fury. The smallest slight is resolved in a deadly duel. There are no rules. The most violent win.

Friends one minute, and in a flash of anger, death and crippling injury the next. I've seen the casualties and the blood that's been spilled on my garb. It's so swift and so silent.

They arrive timid and scared and leave either in a casket or on a stretcher or get turned into killers. It's gladiator school, with this soul sickness passed around like a bad flu bug.

Bodies sprawled, heads cracked open. Beheadings. Knives stuck repeatedly into unsuspecting victims. Blood making pools of red ooze in every corner of this shithouse.

Three-foot-long swords plunged into chest cavities as the victim sleeps. The blade driven right through the chest, the point stuck in the damn floor.

Mad screams shatter the silence as their last breath is stolen.

Cavities are torn open with dull blades to drag drugs from their rectums.

A man's hung in the shower and skinned like a moose. His entrails are splattered all over the shower area. The con responsible for this butchery gathered photos of his work from his lawyer and pasted them up in his cell like centerfold pictures.

Gangs jump on top of a sole figure and stick, slam and beat him with whatever comes to their killer hands.

Making mad dashes into cells, they perpetrate their callous and vicious acts like Green Berets.

They're cowardly but very lethal, hunting their prey like a pack of wolves.

A baseball bat swung with such force that a piece of a man's forehead is chipped and flies off. The victim slumps to the floor. His savage assailant hovers over him angrily and very carefully places his hands over the rounded end of the bat, then powerfully drives the small end through the man's eye. The victim sprawls on the floor as blood gushes and pieces of his brain shoot up like a damn fountain, spraying the ceiling.

This is why I hit like a man condemned to death every time I'm confronted with conflict. The irres-

olute boy turned into a psycho by circumstances . . .
there's no second chance . . .

A screw slips an envelope under my door. Tearing
it open, I see the parole board wants to keep me
under intensive supervision once I'm released. They
want me to report once a week at the police station
and twice a week to my parole officer.

The damn thing goes on to say I must tell them
where I'm going, but I know I won't. I have forty-
eight hours to report on my destination. I know the
stupid law, so go to hell, dickheads.

I'm leaving this mutilating madhouse and I hope
Ury won't forget to carry on the tradition. He still has
a short while, but his hour is coming. He'll have to do
his time on his head and enjoy the trip as best he
can. The crickets can keep him company.

29

The Parole Hearing

A battery of screws appears at my door and says the parole board is waiting to see me. I hate these gutless sewer rats and they'll get nothing from me. I go where I'll go and I won't tell them anything.

I'm being led down the long narrow corridor. We pass through many automated gates and barriers that open on command. I can't wait to see my lawyer. I've never seen him. I wonder what he looks like. I've heard that he's pretty smart, and one who knows everything about prison law and parole head games . . .

The civil dead, that's what I am in this hellish monstrosity, civil dead. Hitler's regime had more civil liberties than this sinister stinkhole. Caesar and the Romans tolerated the Christians more under their laws. Romans—when in Rome, do as the Romans. Living among psychos, I've become a psycho . . .

We come to a stop at a wood-panelled door. Holy mother of Satan, I haven't seen this much wood in a long time. Never been in this part of the prison before. Church pews line clean white walls.

The prison administrators stop and gawk at me. Callous pricks. Haven't they ever seen a con before? They're just as ignorant and classless as the rest of the idiots around here.

WOW, look at that. Dear God. A woman. A damn woman in a long blue dress, curvaceous, voluptuous, with long, well-defined legs and diamond-shaped calves hiked up on thin heels. Long silky ash blond hair and such big beautiful sparkling blue eyes. What a sight for sore eyes to behold. Yet she looks so odd, so out of place. What the hell does she do around here? Sentence calculation? What a wench. I bet she likes to play games like the rest of these dummies.

Looking around, I spot a medium-set, dark-haired gentleman with a cowlick jutting out at the side of a smooth forehead sitting slumped on a pew. He gets up and approaches me, introducing himself as my counsel.

This is David Cole? I don't believe him; I want to see some proof of identification. He looks at me in disbelief, but I'm serious. I've been taught not to trust anyone. I want proof positive before going into the hearing.

Pulling out his identification from the back pocket of his expensive pin-striped pants, he recounts the nature of our brief telephone conversation. He goes on to say he'll do the talking at the hearing. Looking at me curiously, he's questioning the wisdom of his job, I imagine. The legal liar makes money releasing nuts onto the safe streets of his own community. Maybe he'll make a good candidate for my prison. I can even make him the spokesperson for my home video . . .

The lawyer irons out the wrinkles in his dirty brown suit with a shaky, muddied hand and begins to speak into the microphone of my camcorder. Yes, our correctional institutions breed violent offenders and prisons frequently exacerbate their condition. This vigilante wants me to . . . SLAM . . . the camcorder goes off as I slam my fist into his face. His head rocks back as blood trickles down from his eyebrow . . . composing himself, he begins to read from the letter I give him . . .

I follow my lawyer into the brightly lit room and eye the three figures seated at a long rectangular table. Present are two older men in suits, an older woman in elegant attire and a filthy screw, seated in the corner, near the door. I don't like the fact a screw is at my mandatory parole hearing. I've seen enough of these dickheads. I burn my eyes into his before proceeding to one of two chairs facing the three board members.

They look like idiots. I bet they were born with a silver spoon up their ass . . . ha . . . screw 'em . . . an aura of self-importance consumes them . . .

Without any fanfare, my lawyer and I sit opposite the three and he begins to speak as everyone listens to his words of wisdom. I'm not at all impressed with his knowledge, but I'm sure that I'm being released. Any lingering doubts I might have had about that are lifted at this very moment. The haughty board members say I have forty-eight hours to report my destination and advise me I'll be placed on intensive supervision. Big deal. I'll take care of my parole officer first thing. There's no way these idiots can force me to report twice a week to a dumb-ass parole officer. No way.

The lawyer finishes his brief theatrics, and the older gentleman with the thick mane of gray hair who is seated in the center directs a question at me as he adjusts his gold-rimmed glasses on a fat bulbous nose. He wants to know where I plan to go when released.

I remain silent as I stare past his grotesque figure, out the large window and into the parking lot. Hmm, I could write license plates on a pad and run the plate numbers through when I get out of here. Maybe I could set bombs in their engines. Screw them and their stupid questions, I'm not at all interested in talking to these bozos.

With a look of curious amazement, he reiterates

his stupid question a little louder. This one is met with dead silence too. Even my lawyer thinks I'm going to say something, as that look of curious expectancy pasted on his face suggests. I won't say a word to these charlatans. The lawyer gets paid to talk. Then talk. I'll not say a word. I may lose it right here and smash your ugly faces.

The tense silence continues for a few moments and is finally broken when my lawyer nervously tears his eyes away from me and resumes talking anxiously.

His words are echoing around the room as I burn my eyes into the panel members' eyes and try to communicate the message that they're all dead, they just don't realize it. The bitch looks terrified and very worried that this ticking time bomb might come to live next door. I hate these suckers. These are the ones responsible . . .

The young blonde parole representative appears at the prison and says I must sign my parole papers, waiving my hearing for a few weeks until the board has time to evaluate my status. Signing on the dotted line, I never see the parole board again . . .

There'll be no parole for you in *my* prison. I can well imagine you sleep with each other. You're all parties to this torture and to these vicious and deliberate head games. You're all going to pay.

The older-looking lady with the oversized round glasses settled expertly on rotund cheeks and a well-combed bun, keeps staring into my eyes . . . a deep, penetrating gaze. What an annoyance. She's so scared and worried . . . what have they told you, retard?

Clearing her throat, she asks sternly what my plans for release are. Silence . . . deafening silence. They're all looking at me and I can feel the tense silence in the room. I'll say sweet dick all.

They're looking at one another with alarm. I see concern and fear pasted on their pale faces. The jerk at the back shuffles uncomfortably in his hard wooden chair. The junkyard dog is here for security reasons. Pretty flimsy security, if you ask me . . . what can he do if I decide to start smashing skulls?

The lawyer grabs hold of his brown leather satchel and gets up and I follow him out into the narrow corridor. He says the parole board will have to get the papers ready and I'll be out in a few days. Silence . . . he waits for some kind of reply but gets nothing but suffocating silence.

The screws arrive and escort me back down to my hole to wait for the kangaroo court, but I know I have a definite release date set by the board and nobody can touch that baby.

Slammed back in my hole, I feel very good. I'm going to get the bastards and I'll be remembered for time immemorial. I'll become the first serial killer who targets those involved in the justice system. I'm the chosen one. The vigilante man with a powerful message to deliver. Blood and guts will be my means of conveying my message . . .

Blood and guts. Sitting in the prison gym, watch-ing the feature film, I see a hunched figure weaving through the chairs at the front. The dark silhouette is tiptoeing through the rows of chairs. Suddenly, a dark object is lifted high above his head and brought down with great speed. CRUNCH . . . the sound of crushing bone echoes in the large gym. The guy has to be dead. What did he hit him with? A two-by-four? The guy's skull has to be crushed, caved in . . .

They're letting me go. I can't believe it. I've survived this torture dungeon. Mike is dead, Dave was stabbed and had his throat cut, Chris was kicked so hard in the bag he bled from his nose and his ears. Claude had to go to protective custody, Big Paul was stabbed, Davies was beat up, Robert had a sword pass right through him, Nash was hit hard on top of the head with a baseball bat—but I survived. I did it, man. I'll die before I ever come back to this torture pit.

Pacing quickly now. Only a few more days. The

little mouthpiece in the other cell is quiet. He's very lucky. Let him and me go outside and see what happens to his little sharpened toothbrush. I'll slam it in his damn ear and tear his nuts off and stuff them in his mouth. Don't punk me off . . . black . . . I see black . . . like a tight band around my head and a dark cloud veiling my eyes . . .

I know I've gone crazy. I can't help it, man. I may as well do something worthwhile with it. What better thing to do than to kill the ones who drove me insane.

The caldron of water has come to a boil. Picking my metal pot off my Coleman stove by its thin metal handles, I carry it over to the edge of my pit. Peering into its stinking depth, I see my prisoners—haggard, naked, dirty, squirming like worms, shivering, almost comatose—are dying slowly. Some are supine, others shaking, others still lamenting and sniveling. Placing my small shirt on the caldron's hot bluish surface, I toss the boiling water into the pit.

Screaming at the top of their lungs, the captives go stiff as boards. They're in excruciating pain. I walk away with the cacophony of anguish resounding in the night air and pick up my can of gasoline. I really don't give a shit if they live or die anymore. I did what I had to do. I've got one last grand finale to perform.

I'm going to take the warden—that one, writhing, twisting and contorting in agonizing pain—tear out his intestines and hang him up on a streetlight on the outskirts of town with his own corrupt innards. The screws will give him a big funeral procession that will be attended by many involved in law enforcement and corrections.

I'll rent a helicopter and force the pilot to pick up my ammunition, hidden in the bush, and return to the funeral procession being held in the center of town. I'm going to blast away at the pigs. I'll hurl my bombs down on them, fire my heavy-duty automatic weapons into the crowd and kill hundreds . . .

30

An Angel

It's been three days since my parole hearing. I've been waiting, locked up twenty-four hours a day. No yard, no books, no conversation, sitting in this suffocating solitude, twisting, squirming and fighting with myself and staving off the darkness. The tension constricting like a vise around my temples and wrapping itself like a steel band around my pounding head.

The games, the crickets, the mouthpiece and those screws . . . oh, yes, they have it coming to them.

I'm horrified. What the hell am I scared of? I'm frightened of what's become of me. My mind, my whole self is stripped of all sanity, sobriety and sensibility. I'm scared of what I'll do. I know I'll kill these screws. Now they're afraid to let me go, but they must.

Days have crawled into weeks and weeks eked into months and months into endless years. Oh, yes, years.

So many years. So many wasted days. Prime-time twenties wasted in this dark abyss of chaos, misery . . .

You over there, what's your name? You ought to show remorse for your callousness and brutality. The delight you took in harming me, in twisting me, in hurting me beyond repair. Show remorse, you sense- less zombie.

He slinks around like a damn rat. Yes, I'll get my rats and toss them in the cage. Walking casually to my little metal cage, I see Franky is extremely rabid. Opening up the slot, I throw the cage into my makeshift prison as my prisoners shriek in horror. The rats tumble in pools of urine, excrement and muddied glacial waters . . . time for a feeding frenzy . . .

The screws come to my hole in the wall. The pricks are letting me go. I'm being set free. Fear grips me. Anxiety twists my guts and my head starts to swim. Panic washes through my body. This can't be . . . this is unbelievable.

As I'm led down the long hallway leading to the shops, the two screws are joking easily among them- selves. I'm certain the idiots have wagered I'll return within three months. But have they wagered on their lives?

Looking around the dimly lit corridor, flashbacks of years spent traveling down the labyrinth of this stinkhole haunt me. The bastards are a heartbeat away from tasting the fruits of their labor. How many times did I walk down this hellish corridor, only to weld pipes together, nail leather to cardboard or clean the filthy floors? I've worked in just about every shop in this place. Never lasted more than a month in either one of those stinkholes.

Stopping at one of the many thick metal blue doors, the screw twists his huge key in its tumblers and it creaks open. I've never seen this part of the prison before. This is where I'll collect my personal belongings and be led out into the safe streets of their community. Feeling disoriented . . . anxious and pumped.

The screw with the neatly trimmed beard and thin moustache attempts to humor me with some stupid joke, when, turning, I burn my eyes into his ugly face and tell him I'll be seeing him shortly if he doesn't shut the fuck up. Anger surfacing, I want to smash the crooked smile in his twisted face. I hate them. I don't want friendly talk or facades of commonality. I hate their faces and I can't stand what they do to people.

The jerk is startled by my violent response and becomes deathly silent. The tension has become as thick as fog.

The screws pull out dark blue denim jeans and a jacket from a small fenced enclosure, looking to fit me with my size. The damn clothes have to be ten years out of date. I've put on a few pounds over the years, so my clothes are no use anymore, but these damned things are ugly.

Yanking out a faded brown plastic suitcase, the skinny screw advises me to put my personal belongings in the bag.

They pass me white shirts, long blue underwear, old woolen winter tube socks and shirts appropriate for the fifties revolution. I'll look like a hippie with these clothes on my back. Has that much time passed? Feels like it, but I don't think so.

Stuffing the garments into my suitcase, they slam it shut and we stand staring at one another. Breathing heavily, they seem reluctant to spring open the door that leads outside. What are they waiting for? Open the damned doors and let me out. Ready or not, I am coming out.

Pausing, the skinny screw with the thick glasses and slicked hairdo tells me I'll have to be escorted to the finance building to collect my money. I've earned a dollar a day on average while sitting in this shithouse, of which ninety percent was taken away to pay for damages.

When the door leading to the outside ramp opens, I encounter two screws waiting for me in a green sedan. They say I have to get in the car and be driven to the finance building and escorted off the prison property.

Have to? I don't have to do anything. I'm not going anywhere with any of you and I won't jump in any car with your putrid and filthy ilk. I'll go where I want, when I want, with whoever I want to. I'm free . . . screw them and their orders and stupid charges. Up yours.

The screws are startled and begin to panic. The head of security has advised them not to release me if I refuse to go along with them. What a farce. It's my parole date and you assholes have to let me go. I'm going to Kingston.

They try to intimidate, coerce and cajole me to enter the car, but I refuse. They finally agree to let me walk a few feet ahead of the car and say they'll follow me to the finance building located some 200 yards down the road.

The steel gate opens and, approaching the crawling vehicle, I break out in a mad dash for the woods . . . faster . . . voices yelling in the background as wind blows in my face. Eyes wide open, heart beating madly. Looking for my big old tree . . .

Epiphany in the Haven

I'm at the end of my wits as a world of black despair surrounds me. I'm depressed and can't see the use in going on. I want to die—but not before taking a few screws with me.

I've secured a knife from one of the shops and I'm holding it tightly in my hand, waiting in my cell for changeover to be called.

The plan is simple. I will make my way to the central area and start stabbing the screws located in the dome. There are at least four screws there and I figure I can get at least three before I'm gunned down and killed.

Sitting in my cell, I begin to think I'm in hell. If this is what life is all about, I would rather die and end everything right on the spot. I'm very serious— and desperate.

Somewhere deep inside comes the thought that if hell and evil exist, there must be something like heaven and goodness. I have never seen evidence of goodness as far as I'm concerned, but I'm at least ready to investigate the possibility of its existence.

Consequently, I kneel in my cell and pray for the first time in a very long time. I don't believe anything can happen, but I'm very desperate and depressed. I need answers and some kind of reassurance before going out to the dome area to kill the screws and ultimately myself in the process. My prayer goes something like this:

"Dear God, or whatever there is, if there's anything at all. I understand that You can read minds and must surely know what I plan to do this very hour. I see evidence of Satan and evil but see nothing of heaven and celestial joy. If You are up there, I ask You to prove it to me. I'm going to kill these no-good vermin in a few minutes and You know how serious I am. I hope You understand, if You are up there, but I've no choice anymore. Amen."

A few moments pass, then my name is called on the public announcement system.

How could this be? I'm shocked. What the hell could it be? I've not heard my name over that horrible, screechy PA since . . . I can't remember the last time.

Nervous, I place my lead knife carefully in the soapbox, seal the top shut and scramble quickly to my feet as my cell door slides open.

Walking through the dome, the screws tell me that I have a visitor. I can't believe it. I haven't had a visit in well over two years and suspect I'm being set up for an involuntary out-of-province transfer. I've seen them grab many cons and transfer them out of the province.

Paranoid and disoriented, I walk down the long narrow walkway to the visitors' room. When I get there, I'm told my visit isn't to be held in the regular visiting room. Now I'm certain it's a setup. Every nerve in my body is wired and I wait for the goons to pounce at any moment.

As I'm led to a small corridor, my eye catches sight of an elderly lady with thin gray hair, seated on a hard wooden bench. What the hell is this? The screw says this is my visitor. I've never seen this lady before. I have no clue who she is, and certainly no idea what she wants. Curious and perplexed, I move forward a little, as though she could hurt me. I almost laugh out loud, picturing how foolish I must look.

Motioning me to sit down beside her as a mother would her two-year-old son, she's so meek and feeble. She has to be at least sixty years old, but her blue eyes seem so vibrant, so healthy, so alive and gentle.

As I sit by her side, she looks into my eyes and begins to speak words as gentle and pure as a spring breeze. She's so different. Her tenderness, sweetness and compassion hammer me between the eyes.

Still speaking in her gentle and matter-of-fact manner, the little old lady reaches out, places her hand on my forearm and states in a perfectly calm voice that I called her. There's no doubt in her mind and no hint of guesswork in her words. She makes the point-blank declaration I called her and that's why she's here to see me.

I thought I knew about terror. I thought I knew about fear. And dread. But she just said I called her.

Fear, terror and dread seize me from head to toe. How could this be? How could she know? What the hell is all this about? No one heard me pray, and I told no one about my plan to kill the screws. Is this the answer to my prayers? How can this be? My mind racing, body shaking, I can't say anything in return.

My jaw slack and head reeling, I listen in awe as the little old lady talks about the harsh prison conditions in Mexico and how much better off we are in Canada. She goes on to say her cancer is a form of imprisonment from which there's no escape and no hope.

I'm blown away. I can't believe this marvel . . . this . . . this . . . miracle?

Reaching over, I feel her upper arm to make sure I'm not dreaming and she's not some kind of hallucination. She feels soft and warm. Holy shit. This is real.

She says I called her. How could this be? She's certain of it. Not a doubt in her mind. This is not possible, but here she is and this is what she says. And it's true. I did call for help, and here it is, right before my very eyes and ears.

Unable to deal with the little old lady, I excuse myself from her presence, walk hurriedly to my cell, throw the knife out my window and tremble for hours without respite. I abandon my murderous plan . . .

I faintly hear frantic voices begging me to stop, but I'm captivated by the aroma of fresh pine. The fresh smell of damp grass and soaked leaves fills my nostrils. Autumn is in the air. This is so invigorating, breathtaking . . . my mind is racing. The body palpitating. What a rush of adrenaline.

I'm in the thicket now and I can hear voices from the street begging me, threatening me, to come out. What a bunch of idiots. I won't come out. Come and get me if you're man enough, you yellow-bellied scum.

Silence. Silence. Deafening and beautiful silence . . . I love the serenity and solitude of the bush. Several moments pass and the voices stop, so I come out under my own steam. Nobody and nothing controls me anymore, not even reason. Dick all. No inhibitions. A free-for-all and everything goes from now on, free to pillage, murder, loot and rob at random, no holds barred.

As I stroll casually under the hot sun, the little green car follows some fifty feet behind. The screws are paranoid already—and I've just begun.

The finance building looms ahead. Walking into the small building, the screw produces a small piece of paper and requests my signature. He says it's a receipt I must sign to secure my money. I'm not signing anything. The screw says he needs proof that I received my money. What an idiot, I'm not signing anything. Storming out of the building without my money, I make my way toward the highway leading to town.

Epilogue

Ritchy was released from Millhaven in 1987 and has been clean and sober since 1989. He has founded a charitable organization for the prevention of substance abuse and crime and has delivered more than 200 speeches to students. He is working toward his Bachelor of Social Work and has earned his third-degree black belt. As Ritchy says, "I wasn't tough enough."

Ritchy is continuing his writing and works out at the gym to keep fit.

What does Ritchy think about his past? "If I could do it all over again, I'd change everything. But mostly, I wouldn't quit school and I wouldn't take drugs or drink."

Acknowledgments

I owe a big debt of gratitude to Laurence Steven, English professor at Laurentian University, for the tireless work you put into my manuscript. You really made a big difference in the book and in my life. People like you are rare. I am very lucky to have met you and even luckier that you helped. I also want to say a big thank you to Jan Carrie Steven for her tireless support. Jan and her husband, Laurence, are the north's greatest arts benefactors. We are very lucky to have you here at the Sudbury Arts Council.

Many heartfelt thanks go to Patricia Anderson from Helping You Get Published. Without you, I doubt that I would have been published, despite all the great work both you and Laurence put into my manuscript. You performed a real miracle. You took what looked like a languishing pile of papers and helped me place it into the hands of Harper-

Collins*Canada*. That is no small thing. Persistence is key, isn't it?

Don Loney, senior editor at HarperCollins*Canada*, is number one in my book. I couldn't have found a better guy to work with anywhere. You're a good man, Mr. Loney. I'm so lucky to have had the opportunity to work with you. I learned a ton and look forward to selling you the sequel. Keep smilin'. My thanks to everyone at HarperCollins. You are consummate professionals who care for the author. I'm a very lucky guy.

Thank you, Patti Murphy, for your sharp editorial eye. It must have been a real chore to get through the grammatical nightmare I placed on your desk. Thank you for your persistence. Obviously, I'm not the only one who needs persistence to get published. And thank you, Lou, for putting me in touch with your very talented daughter.

A friend, Helene Ethier, planted the seed. You see, Helene, I'm not the only one planting seeds. I thoroughly enjoyed speaking to your students and am honored to have made your acquaintance. We need more teachers—and people—like you.

And my little Share Bear. . . . How can I thank you enough for EVERYTHING? They should hand out gold medals to the spouses of starving artists. If they did, you'd have a wallfull. You're truly terrific and you look fantastic in the pictures. I love you.

I dedicate this book to the memory of my brother Michel Dubé, cousin Louis Longpré and friend Richard Cousineau.

Thinking of Missy, and Joel, who is out there some-where.

With love, Jib, Léa, Manon, Kristin and Brittany—the five rising stars.

I thank my sisters Lisette, Monique and Suzanne for allowing me to write about our family life.

Keep your head up, Erik Michaud. We have a few wrestling rounds to go tonight . . .

Contact the author directly through his website:
http://www3.sympatico.ca/richard.dube